THE ETHICAL LEADER

THE ETHICAL LEADER

Why Doing the Right Thing Can Be the Key to Competitive Advantage

MORGEN WITZEL

BLOOMSBURY BUSINESS

LONDON • NEW YORK • OXFORD • NEW DELHI • SYDNEY

BLOOMSBURY BUSINESS
Bloomsbury Publishing Plc
50 Bedford Square, London, WC1B 3DP, UK
1385 Broadway, New York, NY 10018, USA

BLOOMSBURY, BLOOMSBURY BUSINESS and the Diana logo are trademarks of
Bloomsbury Publishing Plc

First published in Great Britain 2018

Cover design: Eleanor Rose
Cover image © gettyimages

A catalogue record for this book is available from the British Library.

A catalog record for this book is available from the Library of Congress.

ISBN: HB: 978-1-4729-5659-0
         ePDF: 978-1-4729-5660-6
        eBook: 978-1-4729-5658-3

Typeset by Integra Software Services Pvt. Ltd.
Printed and bound in Great Britain

To find out more about our authors and books visit www.bloomsbury.com and sign up for
our newsletters.

CONTENTS

LIST OF FIGURES

1

Creating Value: Why Ethical Leadership Is the Future

Oh, no. Not *another* book about ethics. Not another snowflake pleading with business leaders to be more ethical because, you know, it's the right thing to do and all that. If we were all just a bit nicer to each other, and hugged a few trees, and knitted our own yoghurt, the world would be a much nicer and kinder place.

Well, stuff that. Who cares about being nice? Business is hard, and there is no place for sentiment. The only reason we're all here is to make money. Isn't it?

Actually, this book is all about making money. It shows how behaving and acting ethically, far from being some sort of costly luxury, is actually a powerful source of long-term competitive advantage. Being ethical creates trust. Trust builds strong relationships, and out of relationships comes value. If we can build strong and lasting relationships and create value effectively and efficiently, day in and day out, year in and year out, we will make money. End of story.

Or, not quite. The process is a simple one, but to paraphrase Clausewitz, everything in leadership is very simple, but that does not mean that everything in leadership is very easy. Establishing standards for ethical behaviour and then sticking to those standards and living by them is hard work and requires quite a lot of courage. And ethics itself is not a matter of black or white, right or wrong. It can be hard, sometimes painfully hard, to know what the ethically correct thing to do is.

Sometimes, indeed, it can be too hard. Sometimes it seems easier to accept that the world is an imperfect place, let ethical standards slip and just let things happen. Maybe we won't get caught. If we do, we'll hold our hands up, say we're sorry and promise to learn lessons for the future. Or we'll just say the whole thing is fake news, and pretend it isn't happening.

Stop people in the street and ask them what ethics means to them, and most will tell you that ethics is a matter of right and wrong. Being ethical means following the rules, telling the truth, keeping your promises, doing the right things.

But, of course, this is far easier said than done. Most of us don't follow all the rules, all the time; when the pressure is on, we take shortcuts. A few months ago, driving down a dual carriageway in the West Country, I realized I was late for a meeting. The only way I could get there on time was to break the speed limit. Ironically, I was on my way to a meeting of a police ethics committee, of which I am an independent member. What are the ethics, I wondered, of breaking the law in order to avoid being late for an ethics committee?

Faced with the complexities of ethics in an already complex world, business leaders have an unfortunate tendency to try to sidestep the issue. There is a lot of special pleading – things are different in business; you can't possibly expect us to live up to the same ethical standards as the rest of society; we have to cheat sometimes in order to survive – or even flat-out statements that ethics has no place in business. Luke Johnson's famous article in the *Financial Times*, 'Lies, Damned Lies and Running a Business' argued that firms can prosper only if their leaders are devious, manipulative and unafraid to use deceit as a tactic.[1]

UBER: NEEDING LEADERSHIP HELP

In June 2017 the charismatic CEO of ride-hailing company Uber, Travis Kalanick, was forced by his shareholders to resign. One of the co-founders of Uber, Kalanick became CEO in 2010 and presided over Uber's rapid worldwide expansion. During that time Uber became almost a household name in some parts of the world. Business academics rushed to study the company, describing it as a 'disruptor', using technology to break down the walls of existing categories and transform an industry. Complaints from traditional transport businesses that Uber was wrecking their business were shouted down; Uber was the future.

But behind the scenes, the picture was far from healthy. The culture at Uber was one of win at all costs, or, as the company itself put it, 'always be hustling'.[2] Machismo and aggression were part of the atmosphere. Another of the 'values' was called 'principled confrontation'. When an Uber driver complained to Kalanick about poor pay, Kalanick demonstrated how 'principled confrontation' worked by losing his temper and shouting at the driver. Unfortunately for Kalanick, the video of the incident was posted on the Internet, and went viral. Kalanick apologized for the incident and admitted he 'needed leadership help' to modify his style and change the culture of the company.[3]

Allegedly, bullying and sexual harassment were widespread, and female employees who complained of sexual harassment were silenced. When a woman passenger filed an accusation of rape against an Uber driver, a senior Uber executive attempted to get hold of her medical records in order to discredit her. The executive was later fired, but only when the case came to light in the media.[4] Finally an ex-employee, Susan Fowler, started a blog detailing the experience of herself and others, and belatedly the company took action. Twenty employees were fired for sexual harassment, and more were put under investigation.

Externally, too, the company was running into trouble. Authorities in several American cities as well as in France and Brazil refused to grant Uber licenses to operate. Uber's response was to enter some of these markets without a license, using a software tool called Greyball to spoof the regulators into believing it was not actually in the market. When the transport authorities in Portland, Oregon, found out about this, they reported the breach to the US Department of Justice, which opened an official inquiry.[5]

By now, investors in Uber were beginning to grow worried. So too were senior executives, who feared being tarred with the same brush. After Kalanick agreed to join President Donald Trump's economic advisory council – he resigned soon after – a steady stream of top managers departed

the company, decimating its leadership team. Far from being able to change
the company and reform its aggressive, bullying culture, Kalanick was
struggling to maintain his own credibility. Eventually, the pressure became
too much. Investors, fearing a collapse in the company's share price if any
more scandals came to light, demanded Kalanick resign.

What did Travis Kalanick do wrong? He didn't lie to anyone or break
any promises. Yes, he created an aggressive culture, but no secret was
ever made of this. Nor was the culture of Uber drastically different from
that of Silicon Valley in general, notorious for its male-dominated, highly
competitive atmosphere. Kalanick could argue with some justice that Uber
was no worse than many other companies.

What Kalanick did was let that culture get out of control. The *New
York Times* later called Uber 'a prime example of Silicon Valley start-up
culture gone awry' (although one could also argue that the entire culture,
not just of Uber but of the entire Valley, is fundamentally flawed).[6] When
that culture and its consequences – bullying, sexual harassment, insulting
and abusing employees, stealing medical records, using software to deceive
regulators – was exposed and became public knowledge, Uber's reputation
started to suffer. And for a company like Uber, which has only limited
physical assets, reputation is everything. Losing that reputation has toxic
consequences. Good people no longer want to work for you; innovations
suffer; customer service starts to go downhill; share price begins to slip and
before long the downward spiral begins. Kalanick was closely associated
with Uber's culture, and, once the shockwaves of scandal began to spread,
Uber's shareholders had little choice but to throw him overboard.

Of all the things that went wrong at Uber, it is the internal culture, the
atmosphere of bullying and harassment and intimidation, that was probably
most damaging and has the potential to bring Uber down. A company
staffed by loyal employees who believe in their leaders can usually ride out
most shockwaves.

Would Uber have fared any differently had Kalanick chosen to create a
more inclusive culture that valued all employees equally and emphasized
harmony rather than confrontation? Almost certainly yes. Indeed, there is
a strong argument to suggest that such a culture would have enhanced the
company, making it more resilient and giving it a stronger reputation, and
that the abuses and scandals that destroyed Kalanick's own reputation and
his career could have been avoided.

Modern management theory has largely taken refuge in the positivist paradigm and declaring that management is a pure science and, therefore, anything which cannot be studied scientifically to be outside its purview. You can't manage what you can't measure, the famous dictum goes, and because ethics is one of those things like culture or market sentiment that cannot be accurately measured (you can measure ethical compliance, but that is not the same thing), we are therefore justified in pushing it to one side. Management theorists are supported by some economists, who argue that markets are beyond morality; economics is a pure science, and therefore ethical judgements do not apply.[7] Steven Levitt and Stephen Dubner in their book *Freakonomics* glibly sum up the popular position: 'Morality represents the way we would like the world to work, economics sums up how it actually works.'[8]

Under the positivist influence, business leaders have over the past fifty years or so detached ethics and ethical behaviour from their core business models. Sure, there are codes of ethics, and everyone tries (or pretends to try) to abide by them. But they are a separate subject, not part of the mainstream of business thinking. This is strongly reflected in business school curricula. The University of Exeter Business School, where I teach part-time, has ethics as a core module on its MBA programme; every student has to attend ethics classes. But Exeter is one of the few business schools in the world that does so. Most only offer ethics as an elective subject, meaning students don't have to study it unless they want to (and I've always argued that the people who say they are not interested in ethics are precisely the people who should study it). Far too many business schools don't teach ethics at all.

Why be ethical?

This detachment of ethics from the business core shows a fundamental lack of comprehension as to what ethics actually is. First of all, the positivist idea that science is somehow value-neutral is nonsense. What scientists do affects the lives of us all, sometimes for the good, sometimes also for the worse. Scientists themselves are fully aware of this. The physicists who worked on the Manhattan Project knew that their work could result in hundreds of thousands of deaths, and many of them wrestled with inner demons. One of them, J. Robert Oppenheimer, reportedly told President Harry Truman that he felt he had blood on his hands. Years later, he recalled reactions to watching one of the first tests of the atomic bomb:

> We knew the world would not be the same. A few people laughed, a few people cried. Most people were silent. I remembered the line from the Hindu scripture, the *Bhagavad Gita*; Vishnu is trying to persuade the Prince that he should do his duty and, to impress him, takes on his multi-armed form and says, 'Now I am become Death, the destroyer of worlds.' I suppose we all thought that, one way or another.[9]

The scientists who worked on the human genome project were also fully aware of the abuses to which their work could put.[10] Sir Tim Berners-Lee fought to keep the World Wide Web a public space because he was worried about what could happen if it fell into the hands of a controlling oligarchy. And so on. Ask most scientists about the ethical dimensions of their work, especially those working in applied disciplines, and they will tell you that ethics is very often front and centre in their thinking.

Business is no different, or, rather, it should be no different. Whether we recognize it or not, every decision we make has ethical implications, and that includes business decisions. *All actions have consequences.* Any decision we make concerning our business will impact on other stakeholders in the business. That is a given; there is no getting around it. Our actions as business leaders affect the welfare of those stakeholders, positively or negatively, and this has ethical implications that cannot be avoided.[11]

FACEBOOK: A BREACH OF TRUST

'I'm really sorry', Facebook CEO Mark Zuckerberg told the media in March 2018.[12] He was referring to the scandal raging around Facebook and the consultancy firm Cambridge Analytica, which had accessed the personal data of more than 50 million – possibly as many as 70 million – Facebook users to provide advice to the Leave Campaign during the Brexit referendum, and later to Donald Trump's successful campaign for the US presidency.

Accounts vary as to what really happen. There have been claims that Facebook knew Cambridge Analytica had acquired and was using personal data as early as 2015, but Zuckerberg denies this. According to him, when Facebook learned Cambridge Analytica was holding personal data, it insisted the data should be destroyed. Cambridge Analytica (which has since gone into liquidation) said it had done so, but Facebook failed to verify this. 'This was clearly a mistake', said Zuckerberg.[13]

Not just any old mistake, either, but a whopper, tarnishing Facebook's reputation and leaving users wondering how many other organizations had access to their data. 'This was a breach of trust between … Cambridge Analytica and Facebook', Zuckerberg said. 'But it was also a breach of trust between Facebook and the people who share their data with us and expect us to protect it. We need to fix that.'[14] In another interview he commented:

> I think it's a clear signal that this is a major trust issue for people, and I understand that. And whether people delete their app over it or just don't feel good about using Facebook, that's a big issue that I think we have a responsibility to rectify.[15]

In a hasty attempt to shore up confidence and regain the trust of Facebook users, Zuckerberg announced a raft of measures to protect users' data in the future, acknowledging as he did so that these steps should have been taken much earlier. Yet questions remained about Zuckerberg's own behaviour. The use of unauthorized data by Cambridge Analytica had been headline news on both sides of the Atlantic for several weeks, and it took a long time for Zuckerberg and Facebook to confront the issue and make a public statement. Even after admitting responsibility,

Zuckerberg remained elusive. Although he agreed to appear before the US Congress and, later, the European Parliament, he refused to meet British legislators, even though several million Facebook users in the UK had been affected.

Facebook is one of those once-in-a-generation phenomena, a company that changes not just the business landscape but the world we live in. Like Ford Motors in the early twentieth century, Facebook has had a profound impact on global culture; and, like Ford Motors, it became so enamoured of its own power and importance that it has forgotten that actions have consequences. The belief that social media is a 'good' thing because it links people together and helps them build communities has blinded not just Facebook but other social media platforms as well to the fact that there are people in the world who will use social media for malign purposes. For example, social media companies have also come under fire for allowing their platforms to be used to for hate crimes, and failing to do enough to prevent this.[16]

Again, it is hard to say that Mark Zuckerberg acted in a way which is deliberately unethical. The sin here was one of negligence, of failing to see which way the winds were blowing and take action to prevent Facebook's users from being exploited. Having created these online communities, Facebook has a moral responsibility towards them, in the same way that parents do towards children and employers do towards employees and customers. Facebook must protect its people and keep them from harm.

And if it had done so from the beginning, what would have happened? The Cambridge Analytica scandal would never have occurred, Zuckerberg would not have had to apologize all over the media and appear before Congress, and Facebook's users would be happy and trusting of the platform and loyal to the company. It is not yet certain what the knock-on effects for Facebook will be in commercial terms, or whether users will start leaving the platform in appreciable numbers. But there is no doubt that Facebook is weaker and more vulnerable than it was before this scandal occurred. If nothing else, valuable time has been lost in dealing with the Cambridge Analytica affair, time which would have been better spent developing new and better ways of serving customers and enhancing communities, thus creating long-term value.

For business leaders, ethics is not a nice-to-have. It is a must-have. There are two reasons why this is so. First, ethics helps leaders to project themselves and their businesses. We know the consequences of ethical failure in business; they stare at us from the pages of the financial press every month, sometimes every week. Ethical failures are dangerous. They wreck reputations, destroy value and harm people and communities.

WEINSTEIN COMPANY: AN IMMEDIATE AND INTENSE BACKLASH

Just as Facebook started its climb out of the Cambridge Analytica morass, another once-powerful corporation slipped beneath the surface. On 20 March 2018 the Weinstein Company, which had through its subsidiaries produced 277 films, generating more than $2 billion in revenue and winning twenty-eight Academy Awards, filed for bankruptcy. Its assets were bought soon after by a private equity firm for a fraction of their total worth.[17]

The fall of the Weinstein empire can be related directly to the alleged conduct of its founder, producer and movie mogul Harvey Weinstein. In October 2017, US media reports of more than a dozen allegations of sexual misconduct against Weinstein led to him being fired from his own company. More allegations quickly surfaced, and to date more than eighty women have now accused Weinstein of sexual harassment, assault and rape. Criminal investigations were opened in the United States and Britain.

If Weinstein's colleagues thought that by throwing him under the bus they could save the company, they were badly mistaken. The company faced, in the words of Bloomberg News, 'an immediate and intense backlash'. 'Even longstanding business partners have refused to return the company's phone calls', said one senior Weinstein executive.[18] The company was heavily in debt, but sources of finance began to dry up as even previously friendly lenders walked away. By early 2018 it was clear that the Weinstein name had become so toxic that no one wanted to be associated with it, even though Weinstein himself was no longer with the company. Unable to do deals, unable to raise money, unable to attract talent and by now facing more than eighty legal claims for harassment and assault – some for millions of dollars – the Weinstein Company had little choice but to declare bankruptcy. Its entire business had become unviable, all thanks to a failure of reputation.

Some good came out of this affair, of course. The #MeToo campaign encouraged women – and some men – who had been the victims of sexual predation and violence to step forward and tell their stories, and, as a result, many highly placed abusers in the film world, fashion, sport and politics fell from grace. Some have gone to prison for their crimes. There is more than one silver lining to this particular cloud.

At time of writing, the investigations into Weinstein's conduct are still ongoing. He himself has consistently denied the allegations against him.[19] For legal reasons, this makes it rather difficult to draw conclusions about this specific case. But we can make some general observations about reputation and personal conduct. If you behave in an immoral way towards people around you, especially younger people who depend on you – as some of the other actors and politicians and sports coaches exposed by #MeToo and other campaigns undoubtedly did – then you are risking not only yourself and your own reputation, but every organization you belong to or have any involvement with.

Power corrupts, said Lord Acton, and absolute power corrupts absolutely. Too many leaders allow themselves, too often, to be corrupted by power. They forget why they are in business; they forget the wellsprings of the company's wealth, its customers and its employees. As I wrote in another work, *Managing for Success*, the achievement of power leads many leaders to become arrogant and begin to think only of themselves.[20] They begin to believe their own publicity. In his novel *Bonfire of the Vanities*, Tom Wolfe showed how powerful men begin to believe themselves to be, in his words, 'masters of the universe'. They are bombproof. They can do no wrong. They also begin to enjoy the exercise of power and putting other people down in order to enhance their own power and reputation. In many of the scandals that broke in the wake of the Weinstein allegations, it seems clear that power was a major motivating factor. Sexual abuse, where it occurred, was not just an act in itself; it was also a way of establishing power and dominance over other, weaker people.

Humility is an important part of ethics, at least in the world of business. Remembering that we are not demigods, that we are fragile and vulnerable, that any mistake or misjudgement we make in our private lives can be used as a weapon against us, is vital. As Benjamin Franklin (probably) said, it takes ten years to build a reputation, and ten minutes to lose it. We need a sense of ethics, a strong moral compass, to inform our everyday lives and ensure that as we walk the paths of leadership, we respect the people we encounter along the way. That is how strong reputations are built. Walk the walk.

Sometimes, too, ethical failures cost lives. Business leaders might not be in the position of Oppenheimer's Destroyer of Worlds, but they do have the power of life and death over others. Every day in the UK, someone dies as a result of a decision made by someone in power. They are killed in workplace accidents, or die as result of ingesting hazardous chemicals or fumes from polluting automobiles or factories, or in accidents created by faulty products. Let us not forget, while castigating government for its failures over the Grenfell Tower disaster in 2017, that the fire was actually started by a faulty refrigerator. A fire at another tower block in Shepherd's Bush the previous year was linked to a defective tumble dryer.[21] As business leaders, we have responsibility for these incidents. We cannot simply wash our hands of them, and pretend they are someone else's fault.

OXFAM: TOTALLY UNACCEPTABLE

By any standards, the earthquake that struck Haiti on January 2010 was a horrific disaster. Estimates of the death toll vary between 90,000 and 300,000, and more than 1.5 million people were displaced. International aid agencies rushed to care for the survivors. One of these agencies was the British-based charity Oxfam. Founded in 1942, Oxfam is one of the world's oldest charities working the fields of disaster relief and poverty, and has always enjoyed a high reputation, especially in Britain.

In February 2018, *The Times* newspaper broke the story that several Oxfam workers in Haiti, including the charity's most senior man on the ground, the director of operations, had paid local women for sexual services.[22]

Oxfam itself had been aware of the allegations as far back as 2011. Its own internal report concluded that the aid workers had been preying on women rendered vulnerable in the aftermath of the earthquake, and called this 'totally unacceptable'. The director of operations was offered a 'phased and dignified exit' in order to protect Oxfam's reputation.[23] What seems to have been a separate report was issued to the public in 2011, acknowledging problems of bullying and unsuitable conduct but making no mention of sexual abuse. The latter came to light only in *The Times* report seven years later.

This was bad enough, but when the story broke, Oxfam dropped the ball. In a media interview defending Oxfam, chief executive Mark Goldring accused the press of launching a witch hunt. Oxfam was caring for hundreds of thousands of vulnerable people; surely that was what was most important? 'The intensity and ferocity of the attack makes you wonder', he said. 'What did we do? We murdered babies in their cots?'[24]

Goldring's interview was a case of pouring oil on troubled fires. Within days, the deputy CEO of Oxfam had resigned and Goldring himself had been hauled before a House of Commons committee and forced to make a series of humiliating apologies. The government of Haiti suspended all the charity's operations in the country. More cases of sexual abuse came to light, in Haiti and also in other countries, including Britain. Other charities got caught up in the scandal; Save the Children, another poverty and disaster relief charity, admitted that it too had faced a series of allegations of sexual abuse.

The general public is cynical about business and has low expectations of public services, but it holds charities to a higher standard. I am a trustee of two mid-sized charities in the southwest of England, and I saw how another scandal in the charities sector – this one involving the children's charity Kids Company – reverberated around the entire sector. When one charity fails, it seems, the public tends to blame all of them; if one can be involved in abuse or financial misappropriation, then all the other charities are tarred with the same brush. The Oxfam and Save the Children scandals had the same effect. The BBC reported that more than 7,000 Oxfam donors had withdrawn support from the charity in the aftermath of the revelations in *The Times*, but a separate report by Reuters concluded that the entire charities sector was suffering; Britain was now 'the least favourable country in western Europe for philanthropy'.[25]

As I said, the public expects charities to behave better than businesses, but the Oxfam example highlights a problem that is important for businesses too. As business leaders, we are responsible for the actions of our staff, and their lapses of ethical behaviour hurt all of us. The behaviour of any employee will damage an organization's reputation. As leaders, it is up to us not just to walk the walk ourselves, but to make sure the rest of the organization does so as well.

Again, it comes back to power. Oxfam in Haiti was working with vulnerable, defenceless, traumatized people. Its money and access to life-saving resources gave it power over those people. The director of operations and a small number of other staff chose to abuse that power. Why did not the organization prevent them from doing so? And why, when the abuses came to light, were the abusers not dealt with more harshly? The notion that the scandal could be covered up is absurd. News of something this big was always going to leak out; the only surprise is that it took seven years to do so.

Another lesson lies in how to deal with scandals when they break surface. Mark Goldring's clumsy attempt to deflect attention – 'we murdered babies in their cots?' – arguably did more damage than the scandal itself. When *any* scandal breaks, when any disaster happens, it us up to the organization's leaders to step forward, take responsibility and then take swift and condign action to put matters right. That is the only way that reputation will ever be restored.

It is too early to say what long-term damage Oxfam will suffer from this incident. In the short term, though, it faces a tough mountain to climb as it seeks to restore public and governmental trust, and to persuade the lost donors to return. The charity will also have to replace its leadership team; the deputy CEO resigned as the scandal broke, and Goldring himself has announced that he will leave at the end of 2018. All this represents value lost, opportunity wasted. The time spent repairing the damage should have been spent in finding more and better ways of helping vulnerable people and thus carrying out Oxfam's mission.

Behaving ethically ought to be something that every executive, every manager, every leader is trained to do. If we put people into positions of power and they do not understand the ethical implications of their decisions and actions, then we are putting those people, those organizations and everyone around them at risk.

But there is more to ethics than just warding off danger or mitigating risk. On the other side of the coin, setting high ethical standards and then living up to those standards – walking the walk, as well as talking the talk – can be a very strong and powerful source of positive value. Let me put it as simply and clearly as possible: **being ethical will help you make more money**.

The purpose of this book is to show how this works. As we shall see, putting ethics at the heart of the business model, ensuring that the business and those work for it behave ethically and responsibly, has a strong impact on stakeholders. A business which is perceived as being ethical will improve its reputation with everyone – employees, customers, government and regulators, society at large – and this strong reputation will in turn reap rewards: better customer service, stronger commitment to innovation, happier customers, higher profits and, ultimately, long-term value to shareholders. To put it simply again, ethical business is good business. The ethical leader is also a value-creating leader, whereas the leader who fails to establish a strong moral code and stick to it is a value destroyer.

Being ethical is not just about behaving correctly to the people around us. It is not just about telling the truth, or being transparent, or keeping promises, although those things do matter. But ethics is about much more than that. Ethics also lies at the heart of value creation.

AUSTRALIAN TEST CRICKET: A TERRIBLE SITUATION

'This is a terrible situation', Cricket Australia CEO James Sutherland told reporters. Sutherland was referring to his own investigation into an incident of ball tampering that had taken place in March 2018, during Australia's winter tour of South Africa. Admitting that the incident had taken place,

Cricket Australia, the sport's national governing body, then handed out severe sentences: a nine-month ban for Cameron Bancroft, the young opening batsman who had attempted – rather clumsily – to abrade the surface of a cricket ball with sandpaper, and one-year bans for the team captain, Steve Smith, and the vice-captain, David Warner.[26]

Smith and Bancroft were also banned for two years from any leadership position in the national team. Warner, identified as the prime mover behind the incident, was cast into outer darkness: 'David Warner will not be considered for team leadership positions in the future.'[27] The team's coach, Darren Lehmann, was not held responsible for the incident, but he too resigned his position a few days later.

Australian cricket now faces a long process of rebuilding. The cricketing establishment already had its problems, and a threatened strike by players had only just been averted the previous year. Now, the Australian men's cricket team faces a long process of rebuilding under a new coach and without several of its best players (Smith had been the number-one rated batsman in the world at the time of his ban). Unsurprisingly, Australia suffered a heavy defeat in the final match against South Africa, and lost the series.

But the damage ran deeper than that. 'Baseball is not a matter of life and death', the American baseball coach Yogi Berra once said. 'It's more important than that.' So too with cricket in Australia. Of all sports, cricket is the one most closely tuned to the national psyche. Within hours of the news of the ball-tampering scandal breaking, Australia's prime minister, Malcolm Turnbull, issued a statement condemning the guilty players and demanding strong action. Public opinion supported them. At least one of the team's sponsors withdrew its support, and others, including the national airline Qantas, threatened to do the same.[28] Cricket Australia had been suffering from financial problems for several years. Its leaders need to lose prime sponsors now like they need a hole in the head.

Warner, Smith and Bancroft have all apologized publicly for their misdeeds. Why they did it, we may never know, but it seems most likely that the players simply lost their heads. Desire to win over their strong rivals South Africa, at any costs, trumped their sense of fair play and what in cricket is referred to as 'the spirit of the game'. Some observers grumbled that Cricket Australia had blown the incident out of proportion, and that ball tampering is not that serious a crime. But what ultimately mattered was not the tampered ball, but the reputation of the team, especially among its home supporters who believe very strongly in spirit of the game. To them, ball tampering in order to win a match was unacceptable. They felt that the reputation of Australian cricket – to some extent, even the reputation of Australia itself – had been tarnished, and they reacted with fury. The players, isolated in their own bubble in the dressing room and on the playing field, failed to anticipate this reaction. Now, they are paying for that failure.

Lessons learned

What can we learn from cases like the ones described above? Three points in particular seem to stand out: the notion of *ethical drift*, the equation that power = responsibility and the importance of reputation.

We need to think again about what terms like 'ethical' and 'unethical' really mean. There are some behaviours which are clearly unethical, like sexual abuse, bullying, cheating and corruption. There are others which most of us would agree are ethical, such as kindness, compassion and honesty. In between, however, there is a great deal of grey area where what we do is not obviously unethical but can't really be considered as ethical either.

In this middle ground, it is all too easy to fall into a kind of *ethical drift*, where we take actions or exhibit certain behaviours without really thinking about the consequences of those actions. Uber created a hard-nosed aggressive business culture. That in itself was not unethical, yet that culture led to unpleasant side effects which in the view of many – including, importantly, the company's shareholders – most definitely were unethical. Facebook never intended for its users' data to be harvested and used for political purposes, but it happened all the same.

To be ethical leaders, we must avoid this ethical drift. We need to consider the consequences of every decision we make, large or small. And we need to think what those consequences will be for everyone, not just ourselves or our own organizations, but every person whom our decisions and actions could affect.

Second, we need to remember, always, that with power comes responsibility. Facebook's power stems from its control over the social network; it is the gatekeeper, it sets the rules. That power makes it responsible for the people who use the network, and failure to fully exercise that responsibility leads to the kinds of problems we saw above. Oxfam had control of scarce resources that the homeless people of Haiti desperately needed. The charity therefore had a responsibility to treat these people fairly and with dignity. When a few employees chose to exploit them instead, the result was a ticking time bomb within the organization.

As leaders, we have power over other people. With that power comes a moral choice. We can put ourselves first, use our power to aggrandize ourselves, to get what we want at the expense of others. Or we can use our power with compassion and sympathy for the benefit of other people. In *Kindness in Leadership*, Gay Haskins and Mike Thomas make a powerful case for doing the latter. They argue that kindness is not just a social virtue; it is an important building block of society. Empathy, understanding, warmth towards other people are necessary parts of civilization; without them, it would be everyone for themselves and society would fall apart. They also reference recent scientific work showing that behaving kindly and compassionately towards others makes us feel happier in ourselves, and this has consequences for mental and physical health.[29]

That notion of moral choice is central to the idea of ethics, and we'll come back to that in the next chapter. But for the moment, the point to remember is that there is no escaping that choice. We can outsource nearly everything in business these days, production, marketing, PR, research and development, design, health and safety, human resource management, payroll, accounting; name it, and there is a company out there that will do it for us. But we cannot outsource ethics. We cannot pay someone to be ethical for us, while we carry on doing what we want to do with no fear of consequences.

Finally, there is the issue of reputation, which cropped up in all five of the examples above. It seems quite clear that how we behave in ethical terms strongly affects our reputation, and it seems equally clear that trying to cover up ethical failures rarely succeeds. It took eight years for the ethical failures at Oxfam to break surface, even longer in the case of the allegations against Harvey Weinstein; on the other hand, the Australian cricket team were exposed almost at once, thanks to a television cameraman spotting Cameron Bancroft attempting to tamper with the ball. The lesson is, sooner or later, we will be found out. And when that happens, the impact on reputation can be enormous.

Much depends on how we handle ethical failures when they occur; and another important lesson is, failures will occur. Organizations are made up of human beings, who are fallible. In *Managing for Success*, I suggested a series of red flags or warning signs that can show when there is a risk of failure, including ethical failure, but the truth is that no matter how hard we try, sometimes we will miss the red flags and crash into the rocks. When that happens, how well the leaders of the organization respond is critical in determining the extent of reputational damage. As we saw above, Oxfam fumbled its initial attempt to deal with the crisis, and Facebook was curiously slow in getting out of the starting blocks, with the result that people started wondering why they were so slow and whether they had something else to hide. Cricket Australia, at least, reacted with speed to resolve the situation.

Businesses live and die by their reputations. There is a strong correlation between an organization's reputation and the strength and value of its brand. Stakeholders of all types – customers, employees, shareholders, government regulators, society at large – judge an organization by what they know of its conduct. A positive reputation enhances an organization's ability to function and pursue its mission, while a negative reputation throws up roadblocks. We saw how the Weinstein Company was driven into the ground by its inability to find partners or raise capital, thanks to its toxic reputation.

And reputation in turn depends on the organization's ethics as they are communicated and put into practice. People judge our reputations based on what we have done. Good intentions matter very little; as Henry Ford once pointed out, 'you can't build a reputation based on what you are going to do.'

There is no escaping the need to be ethical. That is why I argue that ethics needs to be built into the heart of every business model. Don't take a decision, then stop and check to see if it is ethical. Get into a position where ethical thinking is present all the way through the decision-making process, so that every decision you make is based on ethical principles.

Of course this is easier said than done, and one of the reasons why people shy away from discussions of ethics is because making ethical decisions can be hard and sometimes involves sacrifices. In this book, we will try to show (a) how the process can be made easier, and (b) why, no matter how hard it is, you still have to do it.

The structure of the book

We shall begin in the next chapter by looking at the concept of ethics. What does it mean to be ethical? Is ethics simply a matter of right and wrong, or is it more complicated than that? (Spoiler alert: yes, it is.) There are several different approaches to ethics, and we will compare these and work out the best approach for leaders to use. Then, since this book is about ethical leadership, in Chapter 3 we will go on to discuss leadership and how the concept of ethics feeds into leadership and affects what leaders do.

In Chapter 4, we shall show how the process of value creation works. Ethical behaviour by the organization leads to positive perceptions and good reputation. Trustworthy firms tend also to be employers of choice, and people who work for firms they trust are more committed and more likely to share the organization's philosophy and goals. This means they work hard and are prepared to innovate in order to deliver superior products and service, which in turn means enthusiastic and satisfied customers. Happy customers lead to strong business performance, which in turn means profitability and value for shareholders. In Chapter 5 we explore how the process works in practice through the *ethical value chain*.

I will use some examples of companies I know and have worked with, notably the Tata Group. I will refer to Tata and its subsidiary companies frequently as we go forward in order to demonstrate how ethical leadership is a 360-degree concept. Ethics has to spread everywhere through the organization; you can't have a business that is partly ethical and partly not. The Tata Group knows this, and has embraced ethics and made it a part of its core business model.

I will also argue that the ethical value chain is a timeless concept. I certainly didn't invent it, nor is it a recent phenomenon. The idea has been discussed for centuries, but in recent years we have drifted away from it. It is time for businesses to rediscover their moral compass, if they want to live long and prosper.

We will then look at two key players in the value chain, employees and customers, and show how their interrelationship works and how they create value. Executives like to think of themselves as value creators. Actually, most value creation happens in the interplay between staff and customers, an arena over which executives often have very little control. Executives are a little like theatre directors. They plan the production, set the stage, work out the supporting props that are needed, tell everyone what they want to happen. But when the curtain goes up, it is down to the actors, and the chemistry and rapport they develop with the audience, that determine whether the performance is successful. In business, the actors are the staff and customers, and it is their performances that determine whether value is created. Ethics and reputation play a big part in determining success.

The wider environment plays a role too. Public opinion matters. In all the cases above, public opinion played a role. Lenders and partners steered clear of the Weinstein Company in part because they were afraid that the company's negative public image would rub off on them. Shareholders forced Travis Kalanick to resign because they were worried that he was too closely associated with the company's increasingly bad reputation in the wider world, and so on. We will talk about the importance of the community as a stakeholder in an organization's reputation, and why ethical leaders pay close attention to what society thinks, and then round off with a brief discussion of the role played by shareholders and the need to rethink the company–shareholder relationship.

Finally, having established some definitions of what ethics means and explored the ethical value chain, we will turn to how ethical leaders make decisions. We will look at frameworks for ethical decision making, and I will suggest a simplified one which can be used quickly and easily. Appendix 1 gives some dilemmas you can use for practice and to assess the utility of these frameworks.

To reiterate a point made earlier, being ethical is not just about mitigating the risks associated with unethical behaviour. We should not do the right thing merely because we are afraid of getting caught if we do the wrong thing (indeed, as the next chapter will show, that in itself could be considered unethical). Being ethical is a very powerful way of building value. To repeat again, being ethical is not a should-do; it is a must-do.

2

Shades of Grey: Understanding Ethics

When I teach an ethics class at business schools, the first question I ask is, 'what does ethics mean to you? How would you define ethics?' I usually get nearly as many answers as there are people in the room. Most people aren't at all certain what ethics means, or have at best a partial definition. The most common answer is that ethics tells us the difference between right and wrong. That is indeed one of the things it is supposed to do, but that is only one facet of a complex subject.

In this chapter, I want to try and take us beyond notions of mere right and wrong and explore some of this complexity. The purpose is to try to demystify ethics and connect it more closely with how we live our everyday lives, and in particular, to emphasize the point that ethics is a matter of personal responsibility. Then in Chapter 3, I will go on to link ethics to leadership and attempt to show how ethics imposes responsibilities on leaders, but also opens opportunities.

What ethics is

The *Oxford English Dictionary* defines *ethics* as: 'relating to morals; treating of moral questions; morally correct, honourable … science of morals, moral principles, rules of conduct, whole field of moral science.' If we turn to *morals*, we find: 'concerned with goodness or badness of character or disposition, or with the distinction between right and wrong; dealing with regulation of conduct, concerned with rules of morality, virtuous in general … founded on moral law, capable of moral action.'

Not terribly helpful, then. The only concrete thing to come out of these definitions is the idea of rules or codes. Ethics would seem to be set of principles that are set for us, and that we are expected to live by, like the codes of ethics that nearly every corporation inserts into its annual report or posts on its website.

The idea that ethics can be codified into a set of rules or principles to which people are expected to adhere has a long history.[1] The Mosaic Ten Commandments are an example of a moral code that also has the force of law; so too is the code of Hammurabi, promulgated in Babylon in the eighteenth century BC. The Chinese doctrine of Legalism, developed by the scholar Han Fei in the third century BC, is another example. The premise of these early codes of ethics and law was that the lawgivers were merely laying down what heaven had ordained.

Philosophers call this the *other-worldly* approach to ethics. In this view, morality is something that exists independently of human beings. We do not make the rules; they are imposed on us by God, or by natural law. That which is ethical is also the desired state of the universe. Some believed this could be achieved naturally. Laozi, the author of the *Daodejing*, argued that leaders should not interfere in the affairs of their followers; leave them alone and they will find the correct, ethical way by themselves.[2] The French Enlightenment philosopher Jean-Jacques Rousseau made similar arguments in the eighteenth century. Others, including Plato and Confucius, concluded that leaders have a responsibility to ensure their followers behave ethically.

The alternative view, the *this-worldly* approach, suggests that ethics are in fact social constructs. Correct behaviour is not ordained by some supernatural force; instead, we as societies choose how we wish to live and what behaviours will and will not be tolerated. This view of ethics also argues that different societies will adopt different codes of ethics depending on their needs; for example, what is agreed as ethical behaviour in China may not be considered ethical in Britain. It is also argued that ethical behaviour changes over time; thus, in the eighteenth century slavery was tolerated in Britain, whereas today it is illegal. This is known as *moral relativism*. In contrast, the other-worldly approach tends towards *moral absolutism*; what is wrong is always wrong, and what is right is always right.

It is hard to say that either approach is entirely right or wrong. People do construct codes of ethics to regulate their societies, as the examples above show. But a comparison of those codes, across the world and over time, show a remarkable similarity between them. Things like murder, lying, theft, cheating and financial fraud are nearly always considered wrong, whereas honesty, compassion and selflessness are nearly always considered virtues to be upheld. The question is, do people abide by these codes?

Slavery may have been legal in the eighteenth century, but that did not make it morally right. In Britain, the issue split the country down the middle with vehement arguments on both sides. Numerous attempts were made to break the slave trade and end slavery over the course of the century, long before William Wilberforce entered the scene. And while slavery may be illegal in Britain today, it still exists. The British government believes there may be 13,000 people living and working in slavery in Britain today, and other sources estimate there are as many as 30 million worldwide.[3] By comparison, around 12 million people were trafficked from Africa to the Americas between 1600 and the ending of the slave trade in the nineteenth century.[4] The law may prohibit slavery, but clearly many people still believe they have the right to enslave others.

TWO APPROACHES TO ETHICS

- *Other-worldly* approach: morality exists independently of humans. Moral values are universal and exist in a spirit-like realm. They are grounded in natural law.
- *This-worldly* approach: denies the spiritual status of moral values. Morals have evolved within human systems, and reflect the rules and norms of society.

This raises another important point; within any set of societal ethical norms, there will be individuals who reject those norms and insist on going their own way. Codes of ethics therefore suffer from a critical limitation. Unless they are also embedded in law, they can be very difficult to enforce; and even then, as the example of slavery shows, the task is still very difficult. In an organizational setting, merely promulgating a code of ethics and expecting everyone to abide by it will not work, even if there are penalties for unethical behaviour. People must *want* to behave ethically, for reasons of either self-interest – treat others as you would have them treat you – or conviction – I will behave ethically because I believe it is the correct thing to do – or both.

And that is tricky, for two reasons. First, how do you motivate people to behave ethically? And second, how do we decide what ethical behaviour is? The leaders can sit down and write a code of ethics, but they are then in effect imposing their own values and beliefs about what is ethical on other people, who may have quite different ideas of their own. Is that right? Is it ethical to impose a set of ethical standards on people against their will? And if we try to get a consensus as to what is ethical, what happens? We find, as I described above, that people have so many different views as to what constitutes ethical behaviour that getting agreement can be next to impossible. The following case study, which I have used when teaching ethics for many years, illustrates the point. (I should add that the details of this case have been very heavily fictionalized, as descendants of some of the people involved are still alive.)

Blackley shipyard: What would you do?

The year is 1931. The place is the small town of Blackley in the northeast of England, population *c.* 10,000. The main industry in Blackley is a shipyard which builds and repairs ships, and employs around 800 people directly. The rest of the town is entirely dependent economically on the shipyard; the yard's employees spend money in the town's pubs and cafes and laundries and markets, enabling these other business to survive.

The shipyard had been founded in the late nineteenth century and had prospered through the First World War, building warships for the Royal Navy. The post-war recession hit the yard very hard, and in 1922 it was nearly forced to close. This caused panic in the town, for it was recognized that without the shipyard, the town itself was not economically viable. There was little in the way of social safety net in those days, and if the yard closed the population of the town would have to disperse to find work elsewhere. A thriving little community would be broken up, and Blackley would become a ghost town.

Into the breach stepped our hero, Arthur Lawrence, a successful stockbroker from London then in his late 20s. He had fond memories of the area, where he had holidayed with his parents and family for many years, and had a great affection for Blackley. Lawrence had done very well in the markets and had money to spend. A well-educated, honourable young man, he was also restless and looking for something to spend his money on, something that would do good in the world. In Blackley he saw his chance. He bought the shipyard, invested his own fortune in it, and built the yard up again, this time making cargo vessels for the merchant marine. Through the 1920s, Blackley prospered.

Then came the Wall Street crash of 1929 and the Great Depression, and the world market for shipping disappeared almost overnight. Orders for new ships were cancelled. For a time the yard survived by doing repair and refit work, but these jobs too began to dry up. By the end of 1931, it was clear that the writing was on the wall. Lawrence and his fellow directors calculated that they had enough money to pay the workforce until the end of February 1932. After that, the money would run out. With no bank willing to lend them funds, they would have no choice but to close the shipyard and lay off the entire workforce, with disastrous consequences for Blackley.

Then, at the eleventh hour, a message arrived. The Ministry of Marine in Romania was looking bids to build two small tankers to service the country's burgeoning oil industry. Building these tankers would keep the yard in work for another year, during which time the economy might improve and the demand for shipping revive. There was one problem: the Romanian government was known to be endemically corrupt, but Lawrence was willing to take the risk. He jumped at the offer like a drowning man seizing a lifebelt, and took the next train to Bucharest. On arrival, he was received warmly by officials of the ministry and made welcome. To his surprise, he discovered that he was the only bidder for the contract.

Everything went smoothly. The Romanian negotiators were happy to accept whatever terms Lawrence proposed. At the end of the second day it was announced that the contracts would be signed at the Ministry of Marine at noon the following day.

At ten o'clock that night, two officials from the Ministry of Marine knocked at Lawrence's hotel room door. Their message was simple and blunt. Unless Lawrence provided a bribe of £20,000, half to the Minister of Marine and half to themselves, before noon tomorrow, the contract would not be signed. There would be no deal. A telegraph line would be held open for Lawrence to contact his bank and arrange a wire transfer, but he would not be permitted to make a telephone call or contact his associates back in Blackley. He had only a few hours, on his own, to decide.

The choice was grim. He could pay the bribe, and hope the officials kept their word and the contract would be signed. If he did so, the shipyard would have work and the business and the town would survive. But he himself would have broken the law; then as now, British law forbade the payment of bribes overseas. If he was caught, he would go to prison, and be banned from ever holding a company directorship again. His career would be wrecked. And he himself would have to live with the knowledge that he had broken the law. Finally, he would have been contributing to and reinforcing the culture of corruption in Romania, where a small number of officials were enriching themselves while the mass of the population sank steadily into poverty.

Alternatively, Lawrence could refuse to the pay the bribe. The deal would collapse, and he would return to Blackley empty-handed and tell his directors and his workforce that it was all over. In two months, they would be unemployed and the community would disappear. He would in effect have sacrificed the shipyard and the town to save his honour.

What was the ethically correct thing to do in these circumstances? What would you do? Think about it, and decide what you would do. (You can find out what actually happened at the end of this chapter.)

Individual ethics

Responses to this case when I teach it are absolutely fascinating. People become very emotionally involved, and I have seen students burst into tears. The last time I taught this case to MBA students, after a vigorous debate, around 80 per cent of the class said they would refuse to pay, with the remainder reluctantly in favour. The previous year, with a cohort of similar size and from very similar backgrounds, the result had been the exact opposite, with around 80 per cent in favour of paying the bribe.

Around the same time I also taught this case to a group of officers in the British armed forces. I had expected them to come down on the side of paying – the culture of the armed forces emphasizes self-sacrifice and being willing to risk yourself to save others – but to my surprise, this group were split exactly down the middle between payers and non-payers.

The reason this case arouses such strong emotions and reactions is that it confounds our notion of what ethics is. There is no black and white here. No matter which decision Lawrence makes, it will be wrong. And yet, on another level, it will also be right. In each case, someone will benefit, and someone will suffer. And each individual sees the problem in a different light, and makes their own choice.

To get some perspective on this case, and on the issue of what it means to be ethical generally, let us look at some of the most important theories of ethics. We shall look at four in turn: deontology, consequentialism, pragmatism and virtue ethics.

Deontology: The difference between right and wrong

Deontology is sometimes described as the ethics of duty. The word comes from the Greek root *deon*, meaning duty or more literally, 'one must'. The most prominent exponent of deontology was the German Enlightenment scholar and writer Immanuel Kant, but versions of deontology can be found in Indian and Chinese thought too; once again, the same ethical principles crop up time and time again in most cultures around the world.

Deontology is about right and wrong, or rather, about Right and Wrong. It tends towards moral absolutism; that is, some things are always Right and something are always Wrong, no matter what the circumstances.[5] Theft, for example, is never justified, not even if one is stealing food to prevent one's children from starvation.

Kant's famous *categorical imperative* stated that we should always act as if the principles behind our actions could be regarded as a universal law. Kant also argued that there are absolute constraints on our actions, the breaking of which is never justified.[6] Nor does deontology take any account of agency. Who you are makes no difference; what is wrong is wrong, whether you are the CEO of a billion-pound company, or the window cleaner.

Kant was also uninterested in the consequences of actions. He was suspicious of terms such as 'good' and 'bad', regarding them as relativistic; nothing in the world, he declared, could be declared beyond doubt to be good. Although the categorical imperative also states that we should treat people not just as a means to an end but also as an end in their own right, it is clear that he regards the outcome of any morally right action as justified. All we need do is obey the natural law, and the correct outcome will be achieved.

The same principle can be found in the *Bhagavad Gita*, the famous Indian text that forms part of a much larger epic, the *Mahabharata*.[7] The *Bhagavad Gita* is largely a dialogue between the warrior king Arjuna and his chariot driver, actually the god Krishna in disguise. Arjuna has been commanded to prosecute a war against a group of rebels, but some of the rebels are also friends and members of his own family. He is deeply unhappy about the prospect of fighting and killing them. At this point Krishna reminds him of his duty. He is the king; his own feelings are immaterial. The fact that his friends and family will die does not matter. He must fight because it is his duty to do so according to natural law.

DEONTOLOGY

- Rules based
- Focus on right and wrong actions
- Consequences of actions are not important

The most extreme example of deontology comes from the Chinese school of Legalism, and I mention it here because it shows how any theory, when taken to its logical extreme, becomes problematic.[8] The brainchild of the statesman and philosopher Han Fei, Legalism is built around two principles: *fa*, the standards to which people must conform and rules with which they must comply; and *shi*, or power. The exercise of power is in the hands of the leader, and his duty is quite simple; to reward those who comply with *fa*, and to punish those who do not.

Han Fei was adamant that the leader did not make the rules; the standards were universal and absolutist ones, embedded in natural law. *Fa* is absolute and universal; *fa* has, indeed, a long, long way to run. The leader is there to see the rules were obeyed, combining the roles of judge and enforcer. No leeway was given to the leader in interpreting the rules, which had to be observed exactly, regardless of consequences.

> Once in the past Marquis Zhao of Han got drunk and fell asleep. The keeper of the royal hat, seeing that the marquis was cold, laid a robe over him. When the marquis awoke, he was pleased and asked his attendants, 'Who covered me with a robe?' 'The keeper of the hat', they replied. The marquis thereupon punished both the keeper of the royal hat and the keeper of the royal robe. He punished the keeper of the robe for failing to do his duty, and the keeper of the hat for overstepping his office. It was not that he did not dislike the cold, but he considered the trespass of one official upon the duties of another to be a greater danger than the cold.[9]

In another instance, the king was receiving visitors when a man ran into the audience chamber and tried to assassinate him. One of the royal guards stepped forward and killed the man before he could strike. The king summoned the guard and rewarded him for saving his life; and then ordered him to be executed for leaving his post without permission.

These two anecdotes highlight some of the problems with deontology. First, if we consider right and wrong to be the only principles that matter, we run the risk of creating injustice in the name of righteousness.[10] Simple humanity would suggest that leaders should be given some leeway in interpreting the rules. Yet, the moment we give that leeway, the whole edifice begins to totter. Right and wrong are no longer absolutes with their roots in natural law, but subjective interpretations. And who then determines what is right, and what is wrong? On what criteria do they do so? And is it ethical for them to apply those standards to other people, who have not had a say in what those standards should be?

In his book *A Theory of Justice*, the American philosopher John Rawls attempted to solve some of the problems with deontology by bringing in safeguards for the less powerful. Rawls argued that any society – or organization – should operate on two principles: first, that every person has a right to liberty, but their freedom should never be allowed to impinge on the liberty of others; and second, that the least advantaged members of society should be protected as far as possible from social and economic inequalities.[11] This is a useful reminder that right and wrong have different meanings depending on one's position in society.

From a deontological perspective, the duty of Arthur Lawrence, the shipyard owner discussed above, is quite clear. The law states that bribery is wrong, and that law is grounded in a principle of natural law, namely, that no one should be allowed to gain an unfair advantage over another. Lawrence should not think about the consequences of his actions; he should obey the law, return home and, if necessary, close the shipyard and make his workers redundant. There will be suffering and hardship, but it will not be his fault. He has done the right thing.

But, Kant also reminds us in his categorical imperative that we should treat other people as ends, not means. And Rawls says that we should not ignore the principle of justice, and should treat others fairly. From this perspective, is abandoning the shipyard and workers and their families the right thing? Does not the leader have a duty to his or her followers? If so, could paying the bribe be considered as morally right, in order to fulfil that duty?

And, finally, sitting alone in a hotel room in the still watches of the night, can you contemplate going home empty-handed and telling your people that their jobs and lives are about to be destroyed?

Consequentialism: The difference between good and bad

In contrast to deontology, the ethics of Right and Wrong, consequentialism is the ethics of Good and Bad. What matters is not the action itself, but its consequences. The correctness of our actions is measured according to the amount of good that results, and how widely that good is spread. One of the first consequentialists was Confucius who, although insisting on the need for rules and structure in society, focused primarily on the outcomes that these rules would generate in terms of greater wealth and happiness.[12]

In the eighteenth century the English economist Jeremy Bentham argued that the principal drivers of human behaviour were pain and pleasure, and that the best interests of the people lay in maximizing pleasure and reducing pain. Bentham recognized the impossibility of making everyone happy all the time; therefore, our goal should be to seek *the greatest good for the greatest number*, a principle that became known as utilitarianism, a kind of subset of consequentialism.[13] John Stuart Mill later defined utilitarianism as 'general happiness', and the elimination of anything that does not produce happiness.

Mill was an absolutist who argued that nothing other than total happiness is desirable. He criticized utilitarianism for its implicit assumption that not everyone's needs can be satisfied and some people will be left behind, and he believed that deliberately consigning some people, no matter how few, to unhappiness was immoral. Most consequentialists and utilitarians, however, tend to be relativist in their outlook. What is considered Good will vary between societies depending on how they are structured and what their values are, and will also evolve over time as society itself changes.

Pure consequentialism focuses solely on the outcome. The actions do not matter; what matters is the result. Machiavelli's doctrine that 'the end justifies the means' is a famous example. Almost at once, though, problems start to arise. If we take this doctrine to its logical extreme, then cheating, theft and murder can be justified so long as we can point to desirable outcome. It is alright to steal money, so long as we give it all away to charity. It is okay to invade other countries if our aim is to overthrow dictators and replace them with democratic governments. It is acceptable to break the law so long as we are doing something that will result in good for others.

And, sometimes it is. It is not acceptable – or so I finally decided – to break the speed limit in order to be on time for an ethics committee meeting, but suppose I had been instead rushing a badly injured person to hospital? Had I saved this person's life by ensuring they received timely medical help, would breaking the law have been justified?

At the heart of the matter is the question of how Good and Bad are determined. Do we always know how to recognize them when they appear? Further, who decides what is Good and Bad? This is one of the things that bothered John Stuart Mill. What right does anyone have to determine what is good or bad for other people? What right do we have to decide what constitutes happiness – or, for that matter, pain – for anyone but ourselves?

CONSEQUENTIALISM

- Consequences of actions are more important than the actions themselves
- Judgement of Good versus Bad
- Greatest good for the greatest number (utilitarianism)
- Ends justify the means

For centuries, small elites of rich white heterosexual males dictated to the rest of the population what was considered good according to their own values and beliefs. Women were, and in some countries still are, banned from a wide range of activities – voting, driving cars, owning property, participating in sport, even travelling on their own – that men were able to freely enjoy, on the grounds that doing these things was not good for them. Homosexuality was banned because it was considered to be a Bad Thing. Slavery was tolerated because it was considered to be economically a Good Thing.

Good and Bad are highly subjective terms, and letting other people decide what is good and bad for us is always risky. People who make these judgements always have an agenda, and we need to know what that agenda is before deciding whether to heed their rules. My Exeter colleague Jennifer Board has written about the paradox of ethics, arguing that in some cases, in order to reform a corrupt organization, it may be necessary to turn a blind eye to some examples of unethical behaviour in order to gain allies and establish a position. Once we have the power to take action, *then* we start cracking down. But we have to have that power in the first place, and achieving it often requires ethical compromises.[14]

To go back to the shipyard case, at first glance it appears obvious that, in order to achieve an outcome that is Good for his workers, Lawrence should pay the bribe. The yard will get the contract, the workers will build the ships and be paid, and the town will stay alive.

However, the consequences for Lawrence himself may not be quite so positive. If it is discovered that he has paid a bribe, his career will be wrecked and he will go to prison. Even if not, he will have to live with the consequences of having committed an illegal act; he will know he did something wrong, even if no one else does. And there is also the impact in Romania itself. By paying the bribe, Lawrence will be contributing to propping up a corrupt and oppressive government that keeps its people trapped in poverty while officials enrich themselves. The shipyard workers will keep their jobs but at the expense of the people of Romania. Is that Good?

Pragmatism: The moral ecology

Right and Wrong, Good and Bad; both give us food for thought when considering what is or is not ethical, but if taken to their extremes, both sets of principles can easily lead us down a moral rabbit hole. Pragmatism, which has its roots in the early twentieth-century thought of John Dewey and William James, argues that trying to separate the means from the end is morally flawed.[15] Both the ends we seek and the means we use to get there have ethical consequences.

Pragmatists argue that rather than adhering to fixed codes of right and wrong, good and bad, and trying to apply them to every situation we encounter, we need to consider each ethical situation on its own merits. It is accepted that we can never know with certainty what the consequences of our actions will be, and therefore a certain amount of trust and faith are required. We make the decisions we *believe* will have the best possible outcomes, knowing that the possibility exists that we are wrong.

This puts pragmatism squarely into the relativist camp; we take each situation as it comes, knowing that different factors will be in play and what is right in one situation may well be wrong in another. John Dewey argued that all ethical behaviour was in effect a kind of practical experiment. In every situation, we formulate a hypothesis about the right thing to do, test it, and, then if it passes the test, put it into practice.

An important concept in pragmatic theory is the notion of *moral ecology*. Whereas deontology and consequentialism use a kind of 'one best way' approach, suggesting that there is only one desirable outcome, moral ecology suggests that many alternatives may be possible. Rather than proceeding down a narrow, tightly defined path towards the Right or the Good, we can evaluate various alternatives that might give us different results.[16] The moral ecology view also argues that the presence of multiple alternatives offers us a better chance of coming to the right ethical decision. Only when decision making is constrained by lack of alternatives do we run the risk of falling into unethical behaviour.

A pragmatic approach to ethics offers us choice; but can too much choice be dangerous? Without greater principles like Right and Good to guide us, how do we determine what is ethical? Pragmatism seems to suggest that we know already what we should do, and it is down to us to find the best way of doing it, the way that will yield the outcome we most desire, out of a choice of many. That assumes, however, that we have sufficient judgement and wisdom to make ethical decisions. And that wisdom, as another colleague from Exeter, Ajit Nayak, points out in his highly perceptive article 'Wisdom and the Tragic Question' in the *Journal of Business Ethics*, is often sadly lacking.[17]

In part, this is because the positivist paradigm has largely killed off any reliance by leaders on the irrational, the emotional and the instinctive, and has left us with the 'you can't manage what you can't measure' approach. Ajit's view is that this leaves managers emotionally crippled and therefore less able to make ethical decisions. Emotion, he declares, is central to wisdom. And it is through wisdom that we see the path before us clearly. A wise leader is one who is not afraid to go against norms and conventions. In a passage that could have come straight from a textbook on pragmatic ethics, Ajit declares that 'wisdom is about recognizing that doing the ethically responsible thing can sometimes lead to acting in ways that violate different ethical norms and values'.[18] In other words, being ethical is far more than just following rules. It requires us to step up and take personal responsibility for our decision and actions.

PRAGMATISM

- Ends and means cannot be separated
- No hard and fast rules
- Each situation is different
- Experimental approach

Using the pragmatic approach on its own is difficult. It requires us to have the necessary wisdom and experience to see the way forward, and the courage to make decisions knowing we might be wrong. Go back and read the Blackley shipyard case again, and then consider what you would do without any reference to principles of good or bad, right or wrong. What would you do?

But for those who have the wisdom and the courage, pragmatism also has much to offer. In the shipyard case, Arthur Lawrence's options would appear to be limited; he can pay the bribe, or not. This was of course part of the plan laid by the corrupt officials. A common tactic in such cases is to isolate the person who has been targeted (alone in Bucharest), cut them off from their supporters (no telegram or telephone available), put them under time pressure (money must be in the bank by noon tomorrow) and then give them a simple either/or choice (pay or walk away).

By moving away from narrow definitions of Right or Good, pragmatic ethics – in theory at least – offers the possibility of opening up other options. Think about the case again. Can other alternatives to simple pay/don't pay be developed?

Virtue ethics: What kind of person do you want to be?

The idea of personal responsibility is highlighted even more strongly in the concept of virtue ethics, usually associated with the work of the ancient Greek philosopher Aristotle, especially his *Nicomachean Ethics*, although very similar ideas can also be found in the teaching of Confucius, especially on the cultivation of virtue.[19] This school of thinking is usually known as virtue ethics.

Aristotle argued that behaving ethically is a matter of *deliberate choice*. All decisions have an ethical component, and therefore we must ensure that we make decisions in a rational way, considering all the factors and thinking the matter through before taking action. Acting on impulse means simply giving way to desire, and we are likely to fall prey to selfishness and other vices. Deliberate choice, on the other hand, requires wisdom and experience, what Aristotle calls *phronesis*, or practical wisdom. It also requires possession of as many facts as possible so that the right decision can be made.

However, even if we make decisions as a deliberate choice, how can we be sure that these decisions are ethical and responsible? The answer, says Aristotle, lies in the cultivation of virtue. He lists a number of virtues that a wise person should possess: courage, moderation, generosity, honour, gentleness, 'friendliness', which I would define instead as sympathy for others, truthfulness and a sense of shame (the latter, says Aristotle, is not a virtue in itself but is a desirable character trait).

Virtues guide and shape our mindset. If we possess these virtues, and refer to them when making decisions, then those decisions stand a far higher chance of being ethically correct because we will be starting out with a predisposition to act in a virtuous manner. In virtue ethics, behaviour and action can be deceiving; what is most important is motive. If a person does not cheat or steal, does that make them honest? Not necessarily; they may not simply have had the opportunity, or be willing to take the risk for fear of being caught. Just because they have not cheated or stolen before does not mean they won't do so at some point in the future.

No, says Aristotle; a truly honest person is someone who will never think of cheating or stealing because they know it is inherently wrong. They do not

---

VIRTUE ETHICS

Deliberate choice
    Collect the facts, then decide
    Practical wisdom (*phronesis*)
    Cultivation of virtue

make a choice about whether to steal or not to steal. The idea of stealing never crosses their mind in the first place.

To sum up, then, in virtue ethics we pause, consider, collect all the facts and then analyse them with reference to our virtues. Of course, this assumes we all have those virtues in the first place, and a cynic might well argue that here is where the theory falls over. People, it is argued, are inherently selfish, greedy and lazy; when making decisions, they will look out for themselves first and the rest of the world can go hang. And, indeed, some people do think like that.

However, there is increasingly powerful evidence that most of us don't, and that the virtues Aristotle talked about may in fact be hard-wired into our brains. In *Kindness in Leadership*, for example, Gay Haskins and her colleagues talk about the notion of our minds being naturally disposed towards kind acts and compassion.[20] Similarly, Paul Zak has written extensively on the part played by oxytocin, a hormone that acts as a neurotransmitter in the brain.[21] Put very briefly, if we are in situations where we are comfortable, the brain releases more oxytocin which produces a feeling of pleasure and happiness. Eating chocolate, having sex and using mobile phones are among the activities which have been identified with the release of oxytocin. On the other hand, if we are uncomfortable, oxytocin emission is reduced, and we begin to feel unhappy or even fearful.

Zak's work has also found that when we feel we can trust the people around us, oxytocin levels increase and there is a corresponding increase in happiness; conversely, if we are suspicious or do not know who we can trust, oxytocin decreases and unhappiness sets in. Studies of primate behaviour among chimpanzees have shown the animals will often exhibit symptoms of trust towards others in hopes of getting a trust response in turn.[22] Humans behave in very much the same way. We trust others in hopes that they will trust us in turn, and the overall increase in trust makes us happy.

It is possible, then, that we do not choose to be virtuous. Confucius thought that virtues were inculcated in the young through family life and education, but it may also be that we are born with a predisposition to virtue because our subconscious mind knows that the cultivation of virtue will make us happy. This is pretty much the argument that is made in the teachings of the Buddha; that virtue is its own reward. Very similar views can be found in the writings of Nietzsche, who rejected codes of morality ('there is something immoral about morality') and the existentialist Jean-Paul Sartre, who argued that objective views of issues like ethics are simply not possible, and that we must instead rely on ourselves; only we can decide what is truly ethical.

If virtue is not a deliberate choice, does that mean that corruption and deceit are? Do some of us deliberately choose to go over to the dark side? The jury is still out on this; it would seem that some people do make a choice, but others may be driven to destruction by imbalances in the chemical composition of their brains. Not everyone finds it possible to be virtuous.

One more time, go back and look at the Blackley shipyard case. Think rationally and clearly about the facts you have to hand (they're all you are going to get) and then ask yourself what a virtuous person would do. What does each of the virtues, kindness, compassion, generosity and so on require of us? What is the virtuous way forward?

Moral responsibility

Having looked at each of the four schools of thought, there is a temptation to try and pick the one that is 'best' and go with that. But, as we have seen, each approach to ethics has its strengths and its weaknesses; and also, it is not entirely possible to escape the demands that each makes of us. The conclusion must be that all four are necessary, and that ethical thinking should blend elements from each.

Definitions of right and wrong are subjective and potentially constrictive, but they are also necessary. 'I want my people to drive fast', a financial services

Table 1 *Four theories of ethics compared*

	Deontology	Consequentialism	Pragmatism	Virtue ethics
Guiding principle	Right or Wrong; outcomes do not matter	Good or Bad; greatest good for the greatest number	Moral ecology; more than one solution possible	Decisions made based on wisdom and virtue
Responsibility				
Strengths Weaknesses	Rules give strong reference point. Strict interpretation of the rules can lead to injustice.	Focus on outcomes frees us from restrictions of rules. Focus on outcomes could lead us to cheat in order to get the right outcome.	Practical, emphasizes needs of given situation. Lack of guidelines can be difficult to know what correct behaviour is.	Focus on self rather than reliance on rules formulated by others. Requires people with requisite amount of virtue and wisdom.

executive once told me, 'but I also want them to drive safely.' Setting out rules is important, if only to give people an idea of where the boundaries lie. That is why codes of conduct and codes of ethics can be useful. Anyone who is tempted to transgress will know what the consequences are.

Good and bad are again subjective moral judgements, but we cannot escape them. The purpose of business, after all, is to create value, and value is created as a consequence of our actions and decisions. As business leaders, we are all consequentialists to a degree. At the same time, we should also be pragmatists. We do need to approach each situation on its own merits, and make decisions based on what will be best at the time. And while we might scoff at the idea of 'virtue' as being old-fashioned and outdated, it looks increasingly clear that the principles of virtue, such as kindness and compassion, may well be ingrained in our psyche, part of the mysterious electrochemical combination of our brain. Being virtuous is natural to most of us.

The Tata Group, which takes ethics extremely seriously, uses all four of the perspectives described above to build and strengthen its own ethical position. Tata has a deontological code of ethics, a document that every member of the organization reads and signs during their induction process. Tata refers constantly back to this document, and operates a zero-tolerance policy; with few exceptions, anyone who violates the code of ethics is ejected forthwith. But Tata also emphasizes consequences. It puts great store by the good it does in the countries and communities where it operates. One Tata subsidiary, the watchmaker Titan, uses a measure it calls 'lives transformed' to show the effect of its social responsibility policies.

There is also a strong element of pragmatism. Rather than having fixed recipes for moral and ethical behaviour and actions, Tata encourages its employees to 'think ethically' so they will know what to do in any given situation. One young accountant, approached by two customs officers for a bribe, did not hesitate; he immediately telephoned the national police anti-corruption unit and helped the officers set up a sting operation, with the result that a few weeks later the corrupt officers were arrested. The first his boss knew of it was when the local papers telephoned him asking for comment. As for virtue ethics, Tata refers constantly back to its own history and the principles of its founders, and looks to them for inspiration and guidance to help them stay on the right path. The result is an organization with one of the highest ethical profiles in the world, and also an extremely powerful and enduring brand.[23]

The most powerful single lesson to take away from the Tata example, and the one common thread running across all four schools of thought, is *moral responsibility*. Being ethical is down to us. We cannot pass responsibility to others. Nor can we use codes of conduct as a crutch. The idea that 'there's no law against it, so let's go ahead', or 'if the code of conduct doesn't forbid it, it must be okay', is nonsense. The examples of ethical failure we saw in Chapter 1 did not always involve legal violations (though in some case they clearly did).

Moral responsibility means assessing each decision, each action and looking at its moral consequences. That is what we must do if we are to put ethics at the heart of our business models.

So what?

Why does all this matter? Who cares whether there are four schools of thinking about ethics, or forty? (Actually, there probably are closer to forty. I picked out just a few of the most important and commonly used ones. Be grateful.) Why is any of this important to modern business leaders?

There are two particular points we need to think about before we move on to a discussion of leadership. The first, which will come as no surprise, is that ethics is a lot more complicated than a lot of us think. Black-and-white situations where ethical decisions are easy to make are, in fact, fairly rare. Much more common are the dilemmas and paradoxes referred to above, like the Blackley shipyard case or the foreign aid case, where there is no obvious right or wrong. Often, any given solution to the problem will simultaneously be both right *and* wrong. And that, of course, presents problems for our ethical leader. How do you get around these problems?

The answer in most cases is that you don't. As we pointed out in *Leadership Paradoxes*, ethical paradoxes are not problems that can be solved.[24] They simply exist, and we have to accept them as part of the landscape. Some ethical problems will always be with us, and will never go away. I make this point to encourage you to move away from the idea that 'ethical leadership' is simply a path we can follow or an exercise we can conduct to make ourselves 'more ethical'. There is not. Being ethical requires us to understand the different dimensions described in this chapter, and learn to think in all of them.

ETHICAL THINKING

- In a given situation, what do you believe constitutes right and wrong action? What do the rules say is permitted/not permitted? What actions would you yourself describe as moral/immoral?
- In the same situation, what do you believe constitutes a good or bad outcome? Who will be affected by your decisions? What will be the positive impact on them? What will be the negative?
- What alternatives exist? If there are no immediately obvious alternatives, can you change the parameters of the situation in order to develop some?
- What does your heart tell you to do? What do you believe, instinctively, you ought to do? Set aside your personal wishes and desires; they do not matter. What, in a perfect world, should you do?

Second, there is the issue of moral responsibility. To put ethics at the heart of the business model, we first have to put it at the heart of our own thinking. Every decision has ethical consequences, and every time we make a decision we need to consider what those consequences would be; whether it is instinctively through innate wisdom, as Ajit Nayak would like, or through deliberate choice, as Aristotle advises, or more probably through a combination of both. The most important lesson of this chapter, then, is focus on yourself. Learn where your own moral compass is, study your own virtues, know what you believe to be ethical and where your red lines are.

Marianne Jennings, professor of financial ethics at Arizona State University, asks her students each year what their own ethical platform is. What is the line beyond which they would not go? She urges them to think about this, and keep thinking about it over and over again as their careers progress. This is part of knowing your own moral compass. If you are firm in your moral convictions, then no threat or demand for blackmail should be able to shake you. This is one of the reasons why firms like management consultants

McKinsey & Company put so much emphasis on ethics; so that everyone is aware of the ethical position, and knows what to do in any given situation. McKinsey reminds its employees constantly of what its core values are, but no one stands over you and checks to make sure you are being ethical. The onus is on you, the consultant, to be ethical; and if you fail to meet the firm's high standards, woe betide you.

The Japanese strategy guru Kenichi Ohmae urged leaders to think about strategy all the time. Don't sit down once a year and conduct a strategic planning exercise, he said; make strategy part of your life. Thinking about strategy is like exercising a muscle; the more you exercise, the stronger the muscle will grow.[25] I would argue that the same is true of ethics. The more you think about ethical principles, the easier it becomes to incorporating them into your everyday decision making. Do this often enough, and after a while you will be thinking ethically without even being aware of it. It will be as natural as breathing.

BLACKLEY SHIPYARD: WHAT HAPPENED?

After a sleepless night in his hotel room, the following morning Lawrence decided to pay the bribe. He wired his bank in the UK, and the money was transferred to Bucharest. Soon after, he met the Minister of Marine and his officials, and contract was signed as promised. Lawrence returned to Blackley and gave the good news to his fellow directors and the workforce, who were overjoyed. However, Lawrence did not tell anyone about the bribe. His reasoning was that, if he was caught, he would take sole responsibility and no one else at the firm would suffer.

Six months later, the British embassy in Romania picked up a rumour that a British shipbuilding firm had paid a bribe to the Minister of Marine in order to secure a contract, and reported this back to London. Soon after, two detectives from Scotland Yard arrived in Blackley to interview Lawrence. When asked if he had paid a bribe, Lawrence admitted it at once, emphasizing that this was his own decision and no one else was involved. He resigned as managing director of the firm and sold his stake in the business to the other directors, and was arrested and placed on trial. As a result of his guilty plea and general good conduct, his sentence was relatively light: two years in prison. He was also barred from being a company director for life. His career was effectively ruined.

Blackley shipyard built the two tankers and delivered them on schedule. By the time the work was completed, the shipping market was strengthening once more, and new orders began to come in. A few years later the expansion of the Royal Navy provided more work still. Blackley continued to prosper after the war until it was nationalized in 1977 and folded into British Shipbuilders.

According to his own testimony, Lawrence remained convinced he had done the right thing. His view was he was responsible for the firm, its people and the town, and that as their leader, it was his role to sacrifice himself for them if need be. He knew he was breaking the law, but considered himself justified. But questions remain? Did he consider the impact his actions would have in Romania? How hard did he try to develop other alternatives? And did he really have no regrets? Was he content that the rest of the world should regard him as a corrupt individual and convicted criminal? Did that really leave no scars?

3

Purpose and Value: What Makes an Ethical Leader?

Just like ethics, there are many competing views as to what constitutes leadership, and nearly as many definitions of leadership as there are scholars studying the subject. Generally, I have followed the mainstream view that the task of the leader is to guide and direct the organization towards its goals. In *Exploring Leadership*, Richard Bolden and his colleagues define leadership as 'a process of social influence to guide, structure and/or facilitate behaviours, activities and/or relationships towards the achievement of shared aims'; a little long, but as accurate a definition as any I have been able to find.[1]

Bolden et al.'s definition is built around two important ideas. The first is the notion of leadership as a *process of social influence*. Leaders do not achieve goals on their own; they need the support and efforts of others. Traditional approaches to leadership assume that leaders gather followers and then give them orders, which the followers then more or less willingly carry out. More recent theories suggest the process is more complex and subtle, and that leaders exercise influence over their followers in a variety of forms in order to draw them together to achieve goals. Alfred Sloan, the legendary chairman of General Motors during its growth years in the 1920s and 1930s, positively insisted that his colleagues debate and discuss his ideas before reaching a final decision. At one board meeting, when it appeared that the directors were ready to nod through one of his proposals, Sloan became mildly irritated. 'I take it you gentlemen are all in agreement', he said. 'Therefore, I propose to put this item back on the agenda at the next meeting, and in the meantime, can we please all think of some reasons why we might disagree?' There are also non-verbal forms of influence such as leading by example.

The second point is the *achievement of shared aims*. Many leadership scholars advise that it is the task of the leader to set the goals, then communicate them to the rest of the organization. For example, in *Leading Change* the influential leadership scholar John Kotter puts 'developing a vision and strategy' and 'communicating the change vision' at the heart of the leader's task.[2] Others disagree, stating that it is important that the vision should arise out of the organization and its values, rather than be imposed from the top. Thomas North Whitehead, for example, paints a picture of organizations coalescing around a set of commonly shared goals:

> Men [sic] seek the society of their fellow creatures, but they need something more than mere physical propinquity. To be satisfying, social contacts must provide for activities performed in common which lead to an immediate pleasure in the exercise of social skills and sentiments, and which are also logically ordered in terms of an ulterior purpose; by these means, stable relationships between persons become established. *The ulterior purpose is to contribute to the future social situation.*[3]

No matter who comes up with the aims and goals of the organization, they must be shared and agreed upon by the organization's members, who are able to identify the organization's goals as their own. Only then will people work willingly to see the goals achieved.

Of course, social influence and achieving shared aims are not always ethical. The concept of dark leadership, much discussed these days, reminds us that leaders can also use their power and influence for unethical and malign purposes.[4] Ethical leadership, in the words of Christian Resick and his colleagues, therefore means 'leading in a manner that respects the rights and dignity of others'.[5] The role of ethical leaders is to ensure that both they themselves and their organizations conduct themselves in an ethical manner. The leader therefore has two tasks:

- To behave ethically
- To persuade others to behave ethically

In practical terms, 'behaving ethically' means building ethical thinking into our business decisions and actions and ensuring that through our work we create positive value for others, while 'persuading others to behave ethically' means harnessing the power of the team so that everyone is working towards that same goal of creating positive value.

This could be seen as a purely consequentialist approach; get the best result no matter what the methods. But the pragmatic approach tells us that the methods and the result cannot be separated. The decisions we take, the behaviours we exhibit, the things we do in the quest to achieve our goals all have consequences and can add or detract from the value we are trying to create. A strict no-tolerance policy with regard to bribery will add to a company's reputation, and people will perceive it as being more trustworthy. In contrast, social network users are now wondering if they really can trust Facebook, and that damages reputation and destroys value.

What, you may ask, is the difference between this and 'ordinary' leadership? The answer is, not much. This is what leaders should be doing, all day, every day. And if they are not doing it, then we should be holding them to account and asking why.

The power of relationships

Two further aspects of leadership are important for this discussion, namely:

- Leadership is distributed
- Leadership is relational

Most people, when they talk about leadership, are thinking of the C-suite. Leaders are directors, board members or senior executives, with big offices and expensive suits and teams of people rushing to carry out their orders. In fact, leadership is distributed throughout the organization. There are leaders everywhere. Anyone who is head of a team, anyone who has other people reporting to them, is a leader. Of course these leaders also have leaders of their own, more senior people further up the hierarchy to whom they report, and even the chief executive of a public company has a leader; the chairman of the board, to whom he or she is responsible and accountable. John Kotter has drawn a distinction between leadership – setting out the vision and goals – and management – getting things done – but while in theory these are separate tasks, in practice, the same people are usually responsible for carrying them out. We lead and manage at the same time.[6]

This is important, because everyone is responsible for ethics. Any organization where, when asked about ethics, people in the lower ranks shrug and say, 'that's the boss's job, nothing to do with me', is in trouble. Everyone needs to take responsibility for their own ethical behaviour; to follow Aristotle, everyone needs to cultivate their own virtues and make their own ethical decisions. Encouraging everyone to take on this responsibility and not shirk it is an important part of the ethical leader's task.

And, secondly, leadership is a matter of relationships. Reiterating the point made above, leaders in isolation achieve very little. In *War and Peace*, Leo Tolstoy talks about how powerless leaders are without the efforts of their supporters. We have a picture of leaders as being in control, guiding the organization through great crises towards their goals, but in reality, he says, most leaders have very little idea what is going on around them and must trust that their supporters and followers are doing what they are supposed to do.[7]

The sociologist and management guru Mary Parker Follett made a similar point in her book *Creative Experience*, arguing that 'control' is in fact an illusion, and that we achieve things only through coordinating the efforts of others.[8] More recently, John Lawlor and Jeff Gold have explained how most leaders operate in a kind of 'fog' and don't really control what they lead.[9]

In *Exploring Leadership*, Richard Bolden and his colleagues offer the view that leadership, instead of being inherent in one person or a group, is in fact a kind of social space encompassing leaders and followers. Instead of being a force or trait or characteristic, leadership is a process. It is something that is done by people working together, a kind of interaction between leaders and followers.

This too is important because we can also conceive of ethics in much the same way. If we lived alone in little bubbles, unable to affect other people or the environment around us by our actions, there might be no need for ethics at all, because we could do no good or harm to anyone. The only person who could feel pleasure or pain is ourselves. But we don't live in bubbles; we live in societies where we are very closely connected to the people around us and actions have consequences. The French philosopher Emmanuel Levinas argued that just like Bolden's concept of leadership, ethics functions through a process of relationships.[10]

All relationships have an ethical component, but also, relationships are the vehicle through which our ethical – or unethical – behaviour affects others. Facebook users were affected by the breach of trust through the relationship they have with the social network; Australian cricket fans were upset because the news of ball tampering affected the relationship they have with their team and so on.

Purpose and value

I am quite a peaceful person and I do not throw things at the television, but I did come close a few years ago when one of the panellists on the BBC series *Dragon's Den* pompously declared that 'the purpose of a business is to make money'. This is such palpable nonsense that I wondered for a moment how the man who said this could possibly be as successful as he appeared to be. I came to the conclusion that he was either (a) drunk or (b) saying something he did not really believe, perhaps to make some sort of point to the people pitching for his investment.

I have sounded off on this subject elsewhere, and I don't intend to return to it in any detail now.[11] I will content myself with reiterating that the true purpose of business is *to create value*. If businesses consistently create value for their customers, and manage the process efficiently and effectively, then they will make money. Profit is not a goal; it is a by-product of the value creation process, your reward for the good work you have done.

Defining your purpose means examining your business to see what value you are creating for stakeholders. Look at it from their point of view. What do they think of you? Why do they regard your business as useful or valuable to them? What does it do for them? If you can answer those questions, then you are on the way to defining what your purpose is. As we will see when we come to discuss the ethical value chain, this is vitally important.

That notion of purpose is highly important, and is central to the concept of the ethical leader. Purpose tells us what the business is for, why it exists and what value is it intended to create. What the purpose of a business might be is not always immediately obvious, and a common error is to mistake purpose for function. Harvard Business School professor Theodore Levitt once famously observed that the railway companies thought they were in the *railway* business and competed against each other. In reality they were the *transportation* business and their real competitors were alternative forms of transport; airlines, road haulage companies and so on.[12]

Today we can make much the same observation about oil companies, who continue to act as if they were in the *oil* industry, whereas in fact they are in the *energy* industry. One day, they will need to wake up to the fact that alternative sources of energy are fast emerging as new competitors. (Sure, most of the oil companies now dabble in renewables, but these ventures are a tiny fraction of their overall effort.) Let us hope, for their sakes and for the sake of stability on world stock markets, that they don't wake up too late.

Another common mistake is to privilege one particular stakeholder group, the shareholders, and define purpose according to their wants and needs. The philosophy of shareholder value maximization, whereby all other needs of the business are considered subordinate to the goal of creating wealth for shareholders, is particularly pernicious in the United States, but it remains common in Britain too, even if it is fading elsewhere. In his book *The Independent Director*, Gerry Brown draws our attention to American research indicating that the majority of directors would be willing to take decisions that would be bad for the business – and by implication its customers and employees – if the result would also lead to greater shareholder wealth.[13]

It is quite true that businesses have a fiduciary responsibility to return value to shareholders, but the law does insist that they do so in a way that is to the detriment of customers, employees or society at large. Logic tells us that a strong and financially sustainable business that enjoys the loyalty of its employees, the trust of its customers and the respect of society at large will, over time, generates more wealth for shareholders than one that gets caught in the fire of its own unethical behaviour and burns out (a point we shall come back to later in this book). The five cases we discussed in Chapter 1 have each resulted in considerable loss of potential value to shareholders. I will say it again; being ethical will help you make more money, especially over the long term.

Back to the future

Value creation for all stakeholders is – or should be – the guiding principle of any business. This too is not a new idea. I certainly didn't invent it, nor did anyone living today. For the past 2,000 years and more, scholars, writers, philosophers, economists and business people have been talking about this very same concept. Let us go back to an ancient Chinese text, the *Daxue*, or 'Great Learning':

> The superior man must be careful about his virtue first. Having virtue, there will be the man. Having the man, there will be the land. Having the land, there will be wealth. Having the wealth, there will be its use. *Virtue is the root, and wealth is only its outcome* [my italics].[14]

In the fourteenth century the Tunisian scholar and writer Ibn Khaldun wrote that 'all markets cater to the needs of the people', and described business people as wealth generators whose task was to ensure that prosperity was spread amongst the people and that they had access to the goods and services they require. A very similar view had been adopted by the religious scholar St Thomas Aquinas, who praised merchants for meeting the needs of the people.[15]

Adam Smith felt much the same way. Over the past few decades, Smith has been hijacked by neoliberal economists who claim – based on misinterpretation of a few passages from *The Wealth of Nations* – that Smith believed that selfishness was a virtue.

Smith believed no such thing. He was a professor of moral philosophy who thought and wrote a great deal about ethics. He is remembered today for *The Wealth of Nations*, but in his own day he was probably best known for his thoughtful and intelligent book *The Theory of Moral Sentiments*.[16] 'Man is endowed with a desire for the welfare and preservation of society', he declared, adding that 'people stand always in need of each other'. He wrote extensively on the principle of 'sympathy', the need to understand other people and their feelings and wants and needs, and long before neuroscience confirmed as much, he argued that people are motivated to act in ways that will earn them the approval of others.

Smith believed that business owners should desire to do good, partly in order to gain approval and to be known in society as good people, and partly out of self-interest; if we treat others fairly and honourably, they will do the same to us, or, as the old saying has it, what goes around comes around. Regardless of which motive is paramount, the purpose of business is still the same: to create value by serving the needs of the people.

Rowntree-ism

One of the largest and most systematic attempts to connect business more strongly with society was undertaken by the Rowntree Management Conferences, mentioned above. Organized by Benjamin Seebohm Rowntree, head of the eponymous chocolate maker from York, the conferences were held between 1919 and 1939, mostly at Balliol College, Oxford, and they brought together a broad spectrum of British intellectual life: business leaders, politicians, labour leaders, natural scientists, psychologists, economists, educators, religious leaders, artists and designers. Hundreds of papers were presented at the conferences over the course of twenty years, and most had a common theme: we are all in this together.

'The old idea that a business is entirely owned by, and should be run entirely in the interests of, those who contribute the capital, must be abandoned', says Arthur Lowes-Dickinson, a senior accountant with Price Waterhouse,

> and the fact admitted, in order to achieve real and lasting success with an absence of friction and disputes, that a business is really a partnership between those who subscribe the capital in whatever form, those who manage the business in its different departments, and those by whose labour, under the guidance of the management, the products are produced and disposed of.[17]

Another speaker, the racing-driver-turned-businessman Gordon England, argued that 'industry is the very lifeblood of civilization, without which it would be impossible for humanity to carry on'.

I would like to suggest that the ultimate purpose of industry ... is to create peace on earth among men of goodwill. Goodwill is the basis of all constructive human effort; there is nothing really constructive that we can accomplish without goodwill ... The whole of industry becomes something very noble, something which is well worth while, and something with which we may be proud to be connected. It is no sordid, money-grabbing, self-seeking effort, but a task for the reformer, the prophet and the pioneer – a task that needs saints and heroes as much as it needs 'sound business men'.[18]

John Lee, formerly a senior executive with the Post Office and a highly respected consultant in both Europe and America, set out his own view of ethics. Industry emphasizes the interdependence of all men and assumes the steady development of man, he said. 'Industry is that which provides for the extensive and the intensive development of mankind in its relation to the use of the products of nature.' Industry makes us better people; it lifts our standard of living, it makes us more wealthy, it produces good things that benefit society, and both the act of work and the act of consumption make us better people. 'What seems to me to be certain is that there has been an expansion of human character, a growth in kindliness of outlook, a desire for justice in reward, and that in the amenities of life for all classes as a whole there has been an advance.'[19]

These are just a few examples out of hundreds of papers. The ideas of the conference were distilled by two of the conference organizers and former Rowntree employees, Oliver Sheldon and Lyndall Urwick. In his book *The Philosophy of Industry*, Sheldon makes the ethical position clear: industry exists only for the service of the community. Both production and consumption are ultimately guided by the community's needs. Goods cannot be produced or sold for which there is no demand from society. There is thus an inbuilt ethical dimension at the very heart of every business; each business exists primarily, if not solely, to fulfil human and social needs. Sheldon refers to this as the 'doctrine of service', meaning that businesses exist primarily to serve their community. Ethics and social responsibility, in Sheldon's view, are not an add-on to business and management. They are part of the core philosophy.[20]

Lyndall Urwick, who went on to become one of the founding fathers of management consultancy and the most important intellectual figure in the history of British management, thought the conferences presaged a new era in business, with old outmoded attitudes swept away and replaced by a new more cooperative and collaborative paradigm based soundly on business ethics:

What new forms will be evolved by business and science working in co-operation it is yet too early to say. Knowledge of the facts is insufficient. Thought and experiment are alike hampered by outworn conventions and traditional practices. One thing is certain. They will bear little resemblance either to the forms of the past or to the imaginative structures which theorists have tried to force upon the world.[21]

I have called this collection of ideas 'Rowntree-ism' because, after studying these papers for the past two years, it seems clear that Seebohm Rowntree, Urwick, Sheldon and their colleagues really were trying to create a new way of looking at the world and connecting business more strongly with society. To some extent they were acting against the advent of the machine age, which they saw as ultimately dehumanizing, disconnecting business from people and turning it into a matter of cogs and wheels and numbers. They were not alone; others were writing along the same lines. Mary Parker Follett warned of the dangers of forgetting that businesses were social organizations, intimately connected with greater society. The French writer Georges Duhamel was alarmed by the erosion of human feeling and emotion in business and in society more general, and the rise of an increasingly mechanical outlook on life.[22]

People of principle

These were not just theoretical ideas. Many business leaders took these principles to heart, and tried to employ them in their own businesses.

We associate the late nineteenth and early twentieth centuries with a grim era of smokestacks and workhouses, extremes of wealth and poverty, brutal authorities and robber barons. This was, of course, the era of the Rockefellers and Vanderbilts, Andrew Carnegie and J.P. Morgan, men who used their power ruthlessly to achieve their goals. But these men were not always popular, and nemesis came for some of them, at least. Public opinion turned violently against the Rockefellers; their business empire was broken up by the government and they were forced to give away half of their billion-dollar fortune to charity in an attempt to restore their battered reputation.

But many other business leaders worked hard to improve the lot of their workers and change the world around them. I will give just a few examples here.

Cadbury: Collaboration in action

George Cadbury and his son Edward, Quaker chocolate makers from Birmingham, set what is still perhaps the gold standard. Today we associate chocolate with tooth decay and obesity, but in the nineteenth century chocolate was seen as a healthy and nourishing foodstuff; milk chocolate in particular as seen as an effective way of getting children to consume milk, ingesting calcium and other vital nutrients.

The Cadburys are remembered today primarily for their philanthropy, including the provision of housing, education and medical care to their workers, but philanthropy was only the tip of the iceberg. The Cadburys regarded their company as part of the community, a collaboration between themselves, their workers and their customers. The bond between workers and owners in particular was very close. George Cadbury himself taught every week in the school he established for the children of his workers. Edward worked closely with the employees themselves, consulting them and listening to their views.

The company established two works committees – one for male employees and one for females – with representation from management, foremen and the shop floor. Members of the committee were elected by their peers, and they had full scrutiny over every major decision the firm took, with the power to reject decisions they did not feel were to the firm's benefit.

The idea of a segregated women's committee might seem anathema today, but things were different then; recall that women in England did not even have the right to vote until 1918, and then only in a limited franchise. Edward Cadbury was quite aware that women employees did not have the same power as men, and he knew that if men and women served on a committee together, the men would simply talk over the women and the latter would have no voice. The purpose of the women's committee was to ensure their voice would be heard; and to further ensure the committee would be taken seriously, he himself served as its chairman from the committee's foundation until he retired.[23]

John Lewis: Sharing knowledge and power

Department store owner John Spedan Lewis went a step further. Inheriting a relatively small London-based company from his father, Lewis devoted himself to building up the company, but in 1927 he suffered a serious accident that kept him away from work for months. Convalescing at home, he made an interesting observation. During his absence, profits and sales continued to rise and the business functioned efficiently and well without him. In a moment of epiphany, Lewis realized that the people who really made the business work, the engine room of its prosperity, were not himself and the executive team but the workers on the shop floor; workers who were paid a tiny pittance compared to what he himself earned from the business.

Lewis resolved that the people who made the business should also share in its prosperity. Profit-sharing schemes were common at the time, but Lewis felt these did not go far enough. As well as money, he argued, true happiness requires that people have access to knowledge and have a degree of control over their own lives. The workers should not just share in the profits, but in the benefits of ownership as well. The result was the John Lewis Partnership, whereby shares were handed over to employees who also, through a series of local, regional and national committees, oversaw the board of directors and influenced business strategy and policy. The Partnership still exists today.

One of the key elements of Lewis's philosophy was the sharing of power and, especially, knowledge. 'The sharing of managerial knowledge is indispensable', he later wrote, 'not only if power is to be shared but also for happiness.'[24] In Lewis's view, happiness was the end game. Businesses exist only to promote human happiness, among employees and customers and in the community.

Sincere: Tradition and values

Chinese entrepreneur Ma Ying-piao, also a department store owner, had a similar view. He founded the Sincere department store in Hong Kong in 1899, where it still exists today. His view was that happiness could best be promoted in part through the provision of high-quality goods and services to spread wealth, and partly through education. Like Cadbury, Sincere had a works school for employees and their children, and Ma came out of his office several times a week to teach in the school. The business was at one and the same time very traditional and very modern, a mixture of Confucian paternalism, Christian values, Western organization and accounting methods and a deep grounding in traditional Chinese culture. The combination proved a potent one, resulting in deep loyalty on the part of both customers and employees.[25]

Tata: What comes from the people goes back to the people

In India, Jamsetji Nusserwanji Tata founded his first business, Empire Mills, on the same principles. Tata paid his employees well and, far in advance of his time, also offered benefits such as sick pay, holiday pay and maternity leave. Later, when establishing the Tata Iron and Steel Company (the forerunner to today's Tata Steel), he built a planned town for his employees, influenced by examples such as Saltaire and the Garden City movement, ensuring that workers and their families were comfortable and had access to health care, education, places of worship and recreational facilities.

Tata did all this not because he was a benevolent patron or because charity made him feel good, but because he recognized, in his own words, that the workers 'were the sure and certain foundation of all our prosperity'. His motto, and indeed one of the mottos of the Tata Group today, is: 'what comes from the people goes back to the people'.[26]

Tata, Ma, Lewis and the Cadburys were looked up to and admired. Nor were they alone; many others followed their example at the time. Indeed, some continue to do so today. Paul Polman, CEO of Unilever, has been lauded

---

We have continued to enjoy prosperity, even with adverse times to fight against. Our relations with all concerned are the most friendly. We have maintained the same character for straight-forward dealing with our constituents and customers. Our productions have continued to be of the same high quality, and therefore command the best reputation and realise the highest prices. ... I mention these facts only to point out that with honest and straight-forward business principles, close and careful attention to details, and the ability to take advantage of favourable opportunities and circumstances, there is a scope for success.

– Jamsetji N. Tata[27]

for his commitment to sustainable growth and his plans to increase the company's presence in emerging markets as a way of assisting development. Ricardo Semler, owner of the Brazilian light industrial company Semco, came to the same conclusion as John Spedan Lewis; his workers were quite capable of running the company without him. His response was to break down the hierarchy and make everyone in the company responsible for their own work plans and budgets. In the UK, in April 2018 Guy Watson, owner of the highly successful organic vegetable producer Riverford Farms, announced plans to give away ownership of the company to his employees, again on the grounds that it was they who created the value and so they should share in the profits.[28]

The concept of moral ecology suggests there are many ways of being an ethical leader. Which path you choose is up to you. Your own ethical principles and priorities will enter the decision, as will the core purpose and needs of the business. As we will see, different stakeholder groups have different priorities, and their needs must be balanced too. You don't have to give away the business to your employees, or devolve responsibility to workers, or commit to sustainability; these are merely some of the ways ethical leaders can put their principles into practice.

Moral courage

Not everyone approves. Some people applaud Paul Polman, but others including some of his shareholders prefer to throw brickbats. His way of thinking about business runs counter to the principle of shareholder value maximization (although over the course of his tenure, Unilever has made good profits and the share price has improved steadily). Polman is challenging the dominant orthodoxy about how and why businesses should be run, and many people are deeply uncomfortable with that.

When Guy Watson announced his plan to give shares in the business to his employees, some were surprised and frankly puzzled; why would Guy want to do this? What was in it for him?[29] Ricardo Semler was branded a maverick by his fellow business leader – a title which he bears with considerable pride – and the idea of employee self-management has been derided as unworkable and impractical.[30] Only in the past few years have some tech firms begun following Semler's example. There have been several attempts to break up the John Lewis Partnership and take the company public, on the grounds that the employee ownership model is old-fashioned and out of date.[31]

Being an ethical leader requires moral courage. Not everyone will approve of what you do. When Robert Owen discovered that cutting his millworkers' hours from fourteen hours a day to ten and a half resulted in reduced fatigue and better health and, therefore, an increase in productivity, he wrote to his fellow manufacturers and advised them to follow his example and reduce hours. The other mill owners responded with fury. How dare Owen cut his workers' hours? How dare he treat them with kindness and compassion? Workers were the lower orders of humanity, and their purpose in life was to be exploited and overworked into early graves. A few years later, Owen's fellow directors tried to remove him from his own company on the grounds that he was spending too much money on educating the workers' children. Small wonder that Owen later became a socialist.

There are risks and costs to being ethical, and there will be times when deals will go sour or contracts will not be awarded because we are not prepared to behave unethically. The Indian entrepreneur N.R. Narayana Murthy, founder of Infosys, shrugged this off: 'I would rather lose a hundred million dollars than a night's sleep', he reportedly said.

The late Ian Rae, who ran a printing and publishing business in Hong Kong for many years, once told me that he knew he had lost business by not paying bribes, but he had also gained business too; people respected an honest man, and wanted to do business with him. Had he paid bribes, word would have

PRINCIPLES OF ETHICAL LEADERSHIP

- Define your purpose according to the value you create for others
- The ends and the means are inseparable in ethical terms; value is created through actions
- Lead by example; walk the walk
- Encourage others to take responsibility for their own ethical behaviour
- Use relationships to convey ethical standards and set the tone
- There is more than one way to lead ethically; how you lead depends on the organization's purpose and the needs of its stakeholders
- Moral courage will be necessary

quickly got around and he would have been marked down as a corrupt man. Being ethical, he said, was risky, but it was a lot less risky than being unethical.

To sum up, the ethical leader is someone who practises leadership in an ethical manner, balancing the needs of stakeholders to create the greatest amount of value and deliver the maximum possible good. Let us look next at how this value is created and delivered.

4

Turning Ethical Principles into Value

Figure 1 shows the *value creation process*, describing the steps through which value is created for various stakeholder groups. As such, it represents half of our ethical leadership model. The other half, the *ethical value chain*, shows what ethical leaders do in order to lead and manage this process. We will come to the value chain in the next chapter. For now, let's take the value creation process apart and see how it works.

The process has its origins in a study of the Tata Group's corporate brand which I conducted around ten years ago.[1] It had been further refined and developed through study of other corporations which have a strong ethical purpose, including McKinsey and John Lewis and also historical examples such as Cadbury Brothers and H.J. Heinz. I will refer to some of these companies as we go along, as well as some other less ethical examples to show what happens when the process breaks down.

It is important to remember that every step in this process must work. The process itself is an organic whole. If one element breaks down or is omitted, then the entire process collapses and positive value begins to turn into negative externalities.

ETHICAL BEHAVIOUR BY THE ORGANIZATION
↓
POSITIVE PERCEPTIONS AND GOOD REPUTATION
↓
COMMITTED AND SATISFIED EMPLOYEES
↓
INNOVATION, EFFICIENCY, EXCELLENCE IN SERVICE DELIVERY
↓
SATISFIED CUSTOMERS, STRONG BUSINESS PERFORMANCE
↓
PROFITABILITY, VALUE FOR INVESTORS

FIGURE 1 *How value is created.*

How value is created

Ethical behaviour by the organization

In the previous two chapters we discussed the ethical principles of leaders and their organizations. However, those principles also have to be in line with the ethical principles of their stakeholders. To put it simply, leaders and organizations need to behave in ways that others expect of them. In Chapter 1, I noted how the public tends to hold charities to a higher standard of behaviour, because they are charities. In the same way, organizations that have good reputations are to some extent in thrall to those reputations; if an ethical lapse does occur, it has more impact because people expected better.

The American fast-food chain Chick-fil-A has long prided itself on its strong ethical principles, and is highly respected by both customers and employees. One of the firm's commitments is to treat everyone – staff, customers and other stakeholder – equally and with dignity and respect.

The firm's principles are in large part derived from the values of the chain's founder, S. Truett Cathy, a devout Southern Baptist. When it emerged in 2011 that a charitable foundation connected to the Cathy family had donated money to pressure groups opposed to same-sex marriage, there was outcry.

The Cathys at first defended their position, which was in line with their own conservative Christian principles, but it became clear that large segments of American society did not accept this. Two cities, Boston and Chicago, announced plans to block further expansion of the chain, and a major business partner terminated its relationship with the firm.[2]

Chick-fil-A reversed its position and publicly reiterated its commitment to treating everyone legally. Did the company sacrifice its own ethics for the sake of its business? Or did it in fact realize that it had made a mistake and move in a matter consistent with ethical principles to rectify the error? Your answer doubtless depends on your own personal ethical viewpoint; once again, there are shades of grey. The point is that expectations are everything. If we do something that we believe is right but everyone around us thinks is wrong, we have choice. We can try to justify our position and hope we are believed, or we can have the humility to accept that perhaps what we believe is wrong and we need to think again. (To make my own bias clear, I deplored Chick-fil-A's original stance on this issue and thought it was highly unethical and out of keeping with firm's stated values of treating everyone equally and with respect. I was glad they changed their mind. You are free to disagree with me if you wish.)

This is not to say that leaders and organizations should adopt a false position in hopes of gaining the affection of the public – that seldom works, at least not in the long term; people are generally pretty good at seeing through charlatans – nor that they should bow to every vapid trend that emerges from social media. But they do need to remember that they are part of a community. Reputation is not just who we are. It is also how others perceive us.

That means communication is important, and that in turn means that ethics should be part of our brand story. The image we present to our stakeholders, to the world, must have ethics and ethical behaviour built into it. Ethics must lie at the heart of the brand. Only if it does will we get the reputation we desire, and only then will we be able to create value.

Positive perceptions and good reputation

Over time, ethical behaviour and actions will be noticed. The communities we serve and in which we operate will behave more favourably towards us, and our reputation for trustworthiness, compassion, generosity and whatever other Aristotelian virtues we exhibit will grow.

H.J. Heinz

Henry J. Heinz was an entrepreneur who started his first business selling food at the age of 8. He founded the H.J. Heinz Company (today part of the Kraft Heinz conglomerate) in 1876. By 1900 it was one of the largest food producing companies in the world.

Heinz's values were centred around the purity and cleanliness of food. He reasoned that good ingredients, properly processed, would keep without the addition of preservatives. His production lines were expensive and, for the day, high-tech, with an emphasis on keeping out impurities and making sure food was safe and fit to eat. As a result, Heinz's products were more expensive, but he reckoned – correctly – that people would pay a premium for the assurance of good quality. Heinz concentrated on providing value for his customers, but he treated his employees fairly and paid good wages, and was very conscious of his company's role as a citizen of the community. 'Humanise the business system of today', he once wrote, 'and you will have the remedy for the present discontent that characterizes the commercial world and fosters a spirit of enmity between capital and labour.'[3]

Adulteration of food and drink by unscrupulous producers was common in the late nineteenth century. Salt could be mixed with sand, or tea leaves with sawdust to bulk them out. Brandy and gin were often adulterated with cheap, dangerous methyl alcohol. Meat and fish were sold half-rotten. Outbreaks of food poisoning were common. A pressure group, the Pure Food Movement, was set up in the 1890s to lobby government for change. Most food producers opposed the movement, but Heinz gave it his public support. The other food producers were outraged, and accused Heinz of betraying them. Heinz responded that the standards the Pure Food Movement was asking for were what his company was already doing. (The movement won, and the Pure Food and Drug Act was passed by Congress in 1906.)

Heinz's support for the Pure Food Movement and his company's commitment to good, healthy food, at a time when it was not always easily available, won him and his company many friends. Heinz was one of the most respected business leaders in America, and his company was widely regarded as a 'good' company. As a result, young people came to him seeking jobs, shareholders were always willing to invest in him and his customers were loyal to his brand.

Lehman Brothers

The bank Lehman Brothers started out with a similar mission of service to the community, lending money to farmers who had no other source of credit to tide them over between harvests.[4] So long as the Lehman family remained in charge, the mission and purpose were maintained. Lehman Brothers had the reputation of being a 'good' bank, one that supported entrepreneurs and treated its customers with fairness and dignity. By supporting companies like United Fruit and Pan Am, Lehman Brothers was making a positive contribution to the American economy and society. Bobby Lehman, the last of the dynasty to lead the bank, worked in close partnership with government regulators and was a strong believer in regulation to curb greed and excess.

Bobby Lehman died in 1969 and leadership of the bank passed to a series of corporate executives, including one who had served in Richard Nixon's cabinet around the time of the Watergate scandal. Gradually, Lehman's mission of service eroded and the company became just another machine for making money. 'There is no Lehman any more', one senior executive mourned.[5] Under the leadership of its last CEO, Richard Fuld, the Lehman

Brothers name became a byword for arrogance, aggression and greed. Profit became an end in itself. Customers were there to be milked. Even other Wall Street banks looked askance at the culture of Lehman Brothers. There was grudging admiration for the fact that at least the bank made lots of money – until it emerged that it had overextended and was actually heavily in debt. In September 2008, Lehman Brothers was forced to close its doors, dragging several other institutions down with it and triggering a worldwide financial crash.

Richard Fuld has stated publicly that he does not know why the US government did not step in to rescue Lehman Brothers as it did several other finance houses. Lehman Brothers' culture of arrogance and toxic reputation may well have had a lot to do with it. Who would want to waste money rescuing people whose only stated objective was to enrich themselves?

The stories others tell

Is that fair to Lehman Brothers? Was everyone in the bank really that greedy? Was that reputation justified? Perhaps not. But that was the reputation nonetheless, and Lehman Brothers did little to counteract the stories that circulated.[6] Those stories made up the bank's reputation.

And here, I think, is an important lesson. Our reputation, our brand, is not determined by ourselves, or at least not solely by ourselves. We are the sum total of the stories other people tell about us. If they tell good stories, our reputation is positive. If they start telling stories about our iniquities and our mistakes, then our reputation starts to go down the plughole.

We can try to influence our reputation by telling positive stories about ourselves, but will we be believed? This is a case where actions speak louder than words. Doing good, living our values, walking the walk, being authentic; these are the things people look for, and it is by our actions that they will measure our worth. A brand story is just that, a story; the story of who we are and what we do.

That is particularly true when it comes to employees. As Mary Jo Hatch and Majken Schultz point out in their book *Taking Brand Initiative*, the employer brand is strongly influenced by the company's wider reputation in the community.[7] The MBA students I teach at various business schools around Europe confirm this. They want to work for companies that are ethically and morally sound, that are committed to making the world a better place, and if they can get satisfaction, they are willing to work for lower pay. They often tell me of their frustration at not being able to find employers whose ethical standards correspond with their own. Perhaps that is one reason why so many business school graduates are now choosing self-employment.[8]

Surveys going back twenty-five years show that companies with a reputation for ethical conduct attract a higher calibre of recruit, and that those recruits are more likely to commit to the company and stay with it.[9] And as we noted above, committed employees generally mean satisfied customers.

Committed and satisfied employees

For a business, one of the most important consequences of having a good reputation is that it becomes an employer of choice. Ford Motors, in the early days after its founding, attracted the best talent in the motor industry because it had a reputation of paying good wages, treating people fairly and being an exciting place to work, at the cutting edge of innovation in the industry. Later, when Ford lost its reputation as a caring employer and began squeezing its staff for extra labour and cutting pay and benefits, the best talent began to migrate elsewhere.

But, I can hear someone asking, why are we are we talking about employees now? Surely the most important thing is the reputation we have with our customers? The customer is king, and all that?

Yes, and no. It is true that customer satisfaction has a huge influence on income and profitability, as we shall see in a moment. But who creates customer satisfaction? The leaders, the CEO and CFO and their team up at corporate headquarters? Or the employees on the ground? Of course, as John Spedan Lewis and Ricardo Semler realized, it is the latter.

The notion of 'customer first' is engrained in most of our business models, but it has been challenged by the Indian entrepreneur Vineet Nayar in his book *Employees First, Customers Second*. Nayar's logic is simple: if you invest in your employees, treat them well, make their work meaningful and show them the value they are creating, you don't need to look after your customers. Your employees will do it for you. If they love their jobs and want to excel, they will go to extreme lengths to create value and please customers.[10]

The principle that if you treat your workers well they will deliver superior customer service is not uncommon in India (though nowhere near as common as it could be). In my view, it is one of the lessons that Indian business has to offer to the rest of the world.

Titan

Titan is India's largest branded watchmaker, and also owns the jewellery chain Tanishq. The company is a joint venture between Tata Industries and the Tamil Nadu State Development Corporation, a public body in the southern Indian state of Tamil Nadu.

Titan was founded on unorthodox principles. Although business logic suggested the company should set up operations in a city such as Bangalore, then the centre of the Indian watchmaking industry, to take advantage of the pool of skilled workers, chairman Xerxes Desai decreed otherwise. In accordance with the principle of contributing to economic development, the company set up its first factory in the small city of Hosur, recruited bright young people from the surrounding villages and trained them to be watch-makers.

The investment in training was expensive. As well as teaching technical skills, the company also had to teach life skills, as many of the villages were remote and impoverished; none of the young people had lived away from home before, none knew how to open a bank account, some had never used a flush toilet.

But the investment paid off. Titan has expanded rapidly and now has factories in several locations in India, and is planning to extend its operations overseas. Its chairman, Bhaskar Bhat, told me he is quite certain that Titan's success is due to the very strong loyalty of its employees.

Why are the employees so loyal? Because for many of them, Titan has transformed their lives. 'I never went to university', one employee said. 'But thanks to my job here at Titan, all of my brothers and sisters have.' Others have left the firm and gone on to start their own businesses, often with financial assistance from Titan. The workers at Titan's factories are utterly proud of themselves and their work. They call themselves 'Titanians' and protect that identity with jealous pride. They regard themselves as custodians of the company's values; when, some years ago, an overzealous manager changed the terms of the company's pension plan without consultation, the workers walked out on strike because they believed this change was not in keeping with Titan's ethos.[11]

Sports Direct

And then, on the other side of the coin, there is fashion retailer Sports Direct.

In 2013, rumours of poor working conditions at Sports Direct's distribution centre, which employed around 3,000 people, began to surface. In December 2015, undercover reporters for *The Guardian* newspaper uncovered a string of offences, including pay below the minimum wage and failure to pay overtime.[12] Staff and former employees almost queued up to tell stories of their experience, including personal abuse and humiliation and being fired for calling in sick. Terrified of losing their jobs, people came to work even when they were seriously ill. According to testimony given before a House of Commons committee in 2016, 110 ambulances and paramedic cars were sent to the dispatch centre over the course of a little over two years; in fifty cases, the illnesses they treated were described as life-threatening. Several were women in labour experiencing difficulties, including one who gave birth in a staff toilet.[13] Chief executive David Forsey faced criminal charges for failing to follow rules on redundancies.[14]

As so often happens in these cases, Sports Direct at first tried to shrug off the issue and pretend it was nowhere near as serious as it seemed. Only as it began to watch its reputation spiral towards the ground in flames did the company take action. Owner and chairman Mike Ashley was forced to make a number of humiliating apologies, most of which were treated with scepticism by the press. Reforms of working practices have been promised, but even two years on, the name Sports Direct is still considered a toxic employer brand. It is safe to say that the only people who would apply to work at its distribution centre are likely to be those who could not get another job elsewhere.

The happy employee

There is, curiously, no empirical evidence to suggest that happy, satisfied workers are more productive, but paradoxically there is plenty of evidence that unhappy workers will engage in all sorts of behaviours ranging from slacking and absenteeism to pilfering, industrial action and sabotage. They also tend not to stay in their jobs very long. The most highly motivated people with the best skills – precisely the ones we should want to keep – are usually the first to go. Meanwhile, the ones who stay are often the ones who are too lethargic to think about leaving, or who haven't the skills and experience to make them marketable elsewhere.

Once the scandals began to unfold around Uber, there was a steady stream of departures from top posts in the company. No one wanted to be associated with a firm whose reputation was turning steadily more toxic. Kalanick's leadership team had been bled white even before he himself was forced out. The new leaders of the company had to rebuild their top team almost from scratch, a time-consuming and expensive process.

It is a lot cheaper to keep a worker than it is to constantly recruit new ones. Over time, too, staff build up banks of knowledge about the company and its industry that are highly valuable. If they themselves feel valued, and if they are working for a company whose reputation makes them proud to be associated with it, they are more likely to stay. Reputation plays a very powerful role in attracting and keeping talent.

And when we can employ top talent and manage them effectively, then pretty much anything is possible.

Innovation, efficiency and excellence

Committed and satisfied employees share leadership's vision of the company's purpose and the value it creates for stakeholders. They know why they get out of bed to go to work every morning; to make the world a better place. They believe their work has meaning.

And that in turn means that they are committed to doing their best, not just for customers but other stakeholders too. They believe in excellent service, and provide it without being asked. They understand the need for efficiency and the avoidance of waste, and take steps to eliminate waste and harmful externalities without needing to be told to do so. They drive corporate performance. All leaders and managers need to do is give them the tools they need and the space to work.

Committed and satisfied employees are innovators. They create new ways of working, new products and services, on the job without the need for costly R&D facilities. *Kaizen*, the Japanese concept of continuous improvement, came from the shop floor at Toyota. In the aftermath of the Second World War, employees were driven by a desire to rebuild Japan's economy and make the country prosperous once more. The impoverished country lacked many of the resources necessary for innovation, so the shop floor workers developed their own system. Rather than seeking big breakthrough innovations, they took incremental, baby steps, constantly seeking to move forward. This inexpensive process born out of necessity helped propel Japan to economic greatness.[15]

The same applies to one of the newest trends in innovation, *jugaad* or frugal innovation, coming out of developing economies. Again, lacking the resources and R&D support of big companies, employees are using their own resources to innovate and create value. The process is inexpensive and results are quick to see.[16] But *kaizen* and *jugaad* would not happen without employees who are motivated to innovate, and have the freedom to do so.

Cadbury Brothers

We have already looked at the culture of collaboration at Cadbury Brothers, and how the company's owners and leaders used works committees to scrutinize decisions and ensure worker participation. The works committees were also engines for innovation. Anyone in the firm could go to a member of one of the committees and make a suggestion for improvement to processes or products.

Cadbury Brothers also operated an employee suggestion scheme, boxes where employees could write down their thoughts on improvement and send them directly to the leadership. Many companies operate suggestion schemes, but not all take them seriously. Employees make suggestions which disappear into the ether, and their ideas are never acted upon or even acknowledged. Not surprisingly, there is quite a lot of cynicism about these schemes.

Cadbury, however, took its suggestion scheme very seriously. Rewards were given to staff who came up with promising ideas, and their contribution was publicly acknowledged. Not every good idea could be acted upon, for a variety of reasons, but Edward Cadbury later estimated that about 20 per cent of all suggestions were rewarded, and around 10 per cent were ultimately put into effect.[17]

Because Cadbury Brothers behaved in an ethical and transparent manner and took the scheme seriously, employees committed to it. Edward Cadbury was emphatic that the workers' contributions over the years had greatly improved the company's reputation and made it far more efficient, resulting in large cost savings. There was a hunger for innovation at the company, a passion for doing things right and doing them well. The consultant Herbert Casson summed up the prevailing culture: 'At Cadbury's, everybody thinks.'

IBM

At IBM in the 1970s, leaders were similarly convinced that their staff were the smartest people in the room. They pointed to a past track record of innovation second to none, and argued that their staff were responsible. Particularly important in IBM's view of itself were the 'wild ducks', free spirits who thought outside the box, dreaming up new ideas and concepts and driving innovation and customer service.

But it was all fiction. That culture had existed at IBM, but it had died long ago. IBM's top leadership had lost control of the culture and lost touch with their employees. The new culture at IBM was one of bullying, intimidation and conformity at all costs. New thinking and new ideas were no longer tolerated; all that mattered now was hitting targets. 'What happened to the wild ducks?' ran the bitter joke among the lower ranks. 'They all got shot.'

The culture of conformity and hitting targets meant that customer interests no longer mattered. No one cared about customer service and quality because there was no incentive to do so. Unable to cope with new technologies such as microcomputers, IBM began to haemorrhage customers and profits. Suddenly, top leadership realized the company they thought they were running was teetering on the verge of bankruptcy. It took three years, thousands of redundancies and a great deal of money to turn the company around, and longer still for it to regain its lost reputation and innovative edge.[18]

Adapt or die

The example of IBM reminds us of what we know already, that companies must continue to innovate and move forward. There is no standing still. There are only two states: growth, or decay.

There are lots of different ways of looking at innovation. There is the bold, breakthrough approach advocated by Chan Kim and Renée Mauborgne in *Blue Ocean Strategy*, or there is the incremental day-to-day approach argued by Patrick Barwise and Seán Meehan in *Beyond the Familiar*.[19] There is the big investment high-tech approach used in industries like pharmaceuticals, or there are *kaizen* and *jugaad* coming from the shop floor. How we innovate matters a lot less than the fact that we actually do it.

And yet, most companies are not particularly good at innovating. An article in *McKinsey Quarterly* in 2008 found that 65 per cent of executives were not confident about their ability to lead innovation. The authors of the article offered three recommendations for driving innovation forward:

1   Formally integrate innovation into the strategic management agenda and the business plan

2   Make better use of existing talent within the organization

3   Foster an innovation culture among employees

'In such a culture', they say, 'people understand that their ideas are valued, trust that it is safe to express those ideas, and oversee risk collectively, together with their managers. Such an environment can be more effective than monetary incentives in sustaining innovation.'[20]

Managing people ethically, treating them with trust and respect, is one of the keys to unlocking innovation talent and creating a culture of innovation. Once such a culture is in place and focused on the organization's goals, the result will be reflected in customer satisfaction and, through this, business performance.

Satisfied customers and strong business performance

When Paul Polman took over as CEO of Unilever and announced that the company would move towards more sustainable products and operations, many analysts predicted disaster. The new measures would be costly and there would be no benefits for either customers or shareholders. It would never work.

The analysts were wrong. The road has not been smooth, but Unilever has proceeded steadily towards its goals, eliminating microplastics from its products, establishing ethical sourcing for its products, working with organizations such as Fairtrade and the Rainforest Alliance to protect the environment and local communities. Sales and profits are rising, and, as noted earlier, the company successfully fought off a takeover bid from Kraft Heinz.[21] Increasingly, there are signs that the public are responding to Unilever's initiatives such as the Sustainable Living Plan, and are taking its products and its ethos to their hearts.

Unilever employs around 170,000 people around the world, and it is clear that they are the real engine for innovation. Paul Polman sets the direction, but it is the workers themselves who generate the vast majority of innovations and carry them out. The same is true at any large organization. The leader declares an intention to innovate; the staff are the ones who actually make it happen. The more committed they are to the organization and its values, the harder they will work to do so.

The same is true of customer service. As marketing scholars such as John Bateson and Valarie Zeithaml have pointed out, customer satisfaction is generated through the interaction between service staff and customers, and the relationships they build. Leadership's ability to intervene in this relationship is limited.[22] Most of the time, the leader sets the tone and directs where the exchange will take place, and then lets them get on with it.

IBM 2.0

IBM today is a very different organization from the one that nearly crashed at the end of the 1970s. No longer a computer maker, the company now calls itself an 'intelligent problem solver'. Its Smarter Planet programme is aimed to 'help companies and systems become much more efficient, intelligent, resilient and reliable'. In the past it has worked with the city of Stockholm to design a programme to reduce traffic congestion and pollution, built a 'green data centre' at Syracuse University that consumes half the energy of a conventional data centre (with corresponding cost savings to the university) and developed a telemedicine initiative in rural America that is cutting down waiting times and resulting in faster, more accurate diagnoses and improved care for patients.[23]

As a result of this approach, IBM has become an employer of choice for young and talented people. Many of my own students would prefer to work for IBM than for any financial institution. That access to talent is what gives IBM its edge in innovation and service, and means it is increasingly become one the first ports of call for any company or organization seeking to build smarter and more resilient systems. And that reputation in turn resulted in global revenues of $79 billion in 2017.

Need I say more?

British Home Stores

The collapse of British Home Stores was one of the scandals of British business in 2016, partly because of the manner in which it failed. Sold by Sir Philip Green's Arcadia Group in 2015 for just £1, the company was already a zombie, one of the walking dead. The new owners, Retail Acquisitions, has no idea how to turn it around. It was discovered that the pension plan now had a deficit of £571 million, and no one knew where the money had gone (although we all thought we could guess). Green refused all responsibility for what happened to the company, but was eventually shamed into helping make up the pension plan shortfall.[24]

Anger about perceived greed and arrogance on the part of BHS's managers obscured the fact that the company had been moribund for many years. 'BHS failed because it lacked meaning and purpose', said one commentator. 'When a brand is meaningful, the workforce is galvanised ... Meaningfulness and relevancy inspires investment and confidence. It instils acceptance and loyalty within communities and households and provides continued reasons to trust in its products and services.'[25]

But when the leadership of BHS lost direction, so did the staff. The engine room of innovation went dark and cold. People turned up to work, did their jobs, went home again. Customer service declined and the range of products on offer never changed. There was, quite simply, no reason for anyone to shop at BHS any longer. The sale to Retail Acquisitions only hastened the company's demise.

Could BHS have been turned around? It is hard to say; times are tough on the British high street, and plenty of famous brands are in trouble. Given commitment, given leadership and values and aspirations, given a committed workforce dedicated to innovation and customers service and building true value, possibly. But one thing is for certain. Without these things, the company had no hope at all.

Happy customers

Getting customers, and even more importantly, keeping them once you have their attention, is the ultimate aim. Customers lead to sales, which lead to profits. There is no escaping that fact, no matter how hard we try. Customers are the primary source of long-term value to the company. In exchange, we must provide something of equal value to them. How well we create value and deliver it determines whether the business itself will survive and thrive.

Being ethical, not just in the way we treat customers but in the way we treat everyone, is crucial. Customers don't like doing business with companies they don't trust. Even if forced to do so for a short time, they will not stay loyal and will be off as soon as a better alternative shows up. Trust is essential to building relationships, and customer relationships are, as any marketing person worth their salt knows, the key to long-term profitability.

Be ethical and customers will trust you. Show yourself to be unethical and they will leave. It is as simple as that.

Profitability and value for investors

And, of course, profitability means value for investors. Not all shareholders are smart enough to recognize this, although one of the smartest of them, Warren Buffett, lists 'demonstrated *consistent* earnings power' among his key criteria for making an investment. The sharks, the greedy investors who prefer short-term cash in hand to long-term value, are still out there circling, but there is a sneaking feeling that their time may soon be up. As profits at the big multinationals dwindle and competition in developed country markets increasingly becomes a game of beggar-thy-neighbour, we are starting to see the emergence of a new paradigm focused on embeddedness in communities and creating long-term wealth.

I won't belabour the point any further. You will have seen by now how the process works. Behaviour and actions based on ethical commitment lead to a strong reputation in the community. When people respect a company and find it shares their own values, they are more willing to work for it, and that willingness to work transmits itself into a passion for innovation and customer service. These in turn lead to customer satisfaction, greater customer loyalty, repeat business and higher profitability, which in turn yields value back to shareholders.

Triodos Bank

Founded in 1980 in the Netherlands, Triodos is a bank with a difference. Far from embracing shareholder value maximization, the bank's ethos is heavily influenced by the early twentieth-century Austrian philosopher and social reformer Rudolf Steiner. Beginning originally as a green investment fund, Triodos grew steadily and has branched out into other banking activities, including savings and retail banking in Belgium, Germany and Spain. Plans to open retail banking operations in Britain are underway.

Triodos is still tiny by comparison with the big banking giants, but its growth has been steady and impressive. The company has strong ethical principles, continues to invest heavily in sustainable businesses and refuses to invest in those whose activities are deemed to be harmful to the public or the environment. Unlike other banks, it also publishes annual lists of loans made and companies it has invested in, so people can see it is remaining true to its principles.[26]

At Triodos, ethics has translated itself into profitability. The bank looks certain to have a stable and prosperous future, based on a strong foundation of ethical commitment to its customers, its staff and the communities in which it trades.

Royal Bank of Scotland

The same could not be said of the Royal Bank of Scotland (RBS) in the run-up to the financial crisis of 2008. Under its notorious CEO Sir Fred 'the Shred' Goodwin, RBS embarked on a string of acquisitions, including Dutch bank ABN Amro and the American Charter One Financial. Many of these acquisitions were criticized for being too costly and not offering value for money. RBS also became heavily exposed to the subprime mortgage market.[27]

Just as at Lehman Brothers, greed and growth became the company's guiding ethos. At a time when concerns about fossil fuel consumption and carbon emissions were rising, RBS decided to position itself as 'the oil and gas bank', lending to petrochemical companies and financing new coal-fired power stations. The company also spent money lavishly on itself, including £350 million on a new headquarters building near Edinburgh and a private jet for the use of the top leadership team. Inside the bank, the culture was one of conformity established through fear. Offices had to look tidy; special filing cabinets with sloping tops were purchased so staff could not put anything on top of them. Insiders spoke of bullying and infighting amongst managers and staff morale spiralling downward.

It couldn't last, and it didn't. The 2008 financial crisis brought the house of cards tumbling down. The British government stepped in and rescued RBS in October of that year, and Goodwin resigned. He was subsequently pilloried in the British press and by politicians of all parties, and later stripped of his knighthood. He remains one of the most infamous figures in British banking, his name in the public mind synonymous with the banking crash.

Of course, Goodwin is not fully to blame for the disaster, just as Fuld did not single-handedly cause the crash of Lehman Brothers. As leaders, they take responsibility for the failure, and their own role must of course be scrutinized. But a culture of greed and reckless expansion had existed at RBS before Goodwin came to power. Shareholders failed to check that culture, or to act decisively to change the bank's course before it was too late. One of the lessons of RBS is this: companies have an ethical responsibility to shareholders, but shareholders have a reciprocal ethical responsibility to those companies whose capital they own, to ensure they are managed wisely and well.

ETHICS AND PROFIT

The notion of profiting from ethical behaviour makes some people uncomfortable. When I proposed this idea to an academic colleague a couple of years ago, he became quite irate. People shouldn't be ethical in order to make a profit, he insisted; they should be ethical because it is the right thing to do. Profit and ethics should be kept completely separate, and should not even be discussed in the same breath.

In part, this view is rooted in the old-fashioned religious view that 'profit' is itself immoral, that by making a profit we are taking something away from other people that is not rightfully ours. Actually, there is quite a strong strain of religious teaching that runs counter to this view. St Thomas

Aquinas thought that profit was a merchant's reward for taking risks, and the Syrian Muslim scholar Abu Fadl al-Dimashqi argued that profit, so long as it was lawfully gained, was pleasing in the eyes of God. Profit *is* immoral if we lie, cheat or deceive others in order to get it, but so long as we are creating value for other people in exchange, then we are fairly entitled to a profit. As Aquinas again reminds us, it is then up to us to spend or use that profit in a moral and honest way.

How the process works

For me, the company that best demonstrates how the process works is the Tata Group. As I mentioned above, the basis for this model comes from my work with Tata a number of years ago, and it seems appropriate to use Tata as an example now.

As mentioned earlier, the Tata Group was founded in 1868 with the establishment of Empress Mills by the entrepreneur Jamsetji N. Tata. Other businesses engaged in steel making, power generation, hotels and, later, cars, airlines, retail and consumer goods, communications, chemicals and consultancy followed. Today the Group numbers over a hundred separate businesses, all pulled together under the umbrella of Tata Sons, headquartered in Mumbai. Tata Sons in turn is two-thirds owned by a group of charitable trusts set up by various members of the Tata family over the years. The Tata family themselves own only a small stake in Tata Sons.

Again as noted, Tata has consistently stuck to its values and mission. Jamsetji Tata favoured Indian independence from Britain, and argued that to be strong, a free India would need a strong economy. His business ventures were made with this aim. For example, his decision to found the famous Taj Mahal Palace Hotel in Mumbai was made with a view to attracting foreign direct investment. Foreign industrialists and bankers would be more likely to come to India, he reasoned, if they had comfortable accommodation once they arrived.

Over the century and a half of its existence, Tata has established a reputation based on three values: trust, reliability and commitment to the community. Tata's public commitment to integrity, its zero-tolerance policy on corruption in a country where corruption remains a serious problem and the fact that its leaders really do walk the walk and live up to their word mean the company are widely admired. It has a reputation for reliability and keeping its word; its products are of good quality and any defects or lapses are repaired or replaced immediately and without quibble. Service at its hotels is of an extremely high standard.

And finally, Jamsetji Tata's original mission of service, to India and other countries where the group operates, remains very strong. Tata earns profits from its business operations, but it spends much of them on helping others. At Jamshedpur, home of the original steel mill, Tata Steel provides free health care and education to villagers in more than 600 rural communities nearby. At Pune, the headquarters of Tata Motors, the company is involved in numerous outreach programmes, including a major investment in helping women start their own businesses and become economically self-sufficient.

That reputation is a source of pride in India, and you can see it everywhere you go. Once, at lunch in a hotel owned by one of Tata's rivals, I mentioned to the headwaiter that I was writing a book about Tata. His eyes widened. 'What a great company', he enthused. He must have told everyone in the kitchen, because the waiter who brought my lunch a few minutes later asked if it was true I was writing about Tata. Yes, I said. 'Oh, sir', he said quietly. 'That must be such a great honour.'

A few days later, changing planes at Kolkata, a very severe and unsmiling security guard took my passport and asked my destination. Jamshedpur, I said, referring to the home of Tata Steel. His demeanour changed at once. 'Ah,

Jamshedpur!' he said, handing my passport back with a grin. 'Have a good journey.'

That reputation means that Tata is an employer of choice in India. At Jamshedpur, I met people whose families had worked for the company for five generations. They had no desire to work anywhere else; Tata was their home. Young graduates of business schools and IIMs rush to apply for jobs at Tata, even though they know managerial wages are significantly lower than in some other firms. The people who come to work for Tata really want to work there. They believe in Tata, thanks to that shining reputation.

That means they are dedicated to their jobs. In all my time studying the Tata Group, I never met anyone who was not 100 per cent committed to their work. They believe passionately in customer service. And in 2008, Tata was named one of the ten most innovative companies in the world. Whether it is the world's thinnest watch, or the micro car that can be made and sold for less than £2,000, or another car powered by compressed air, or a new and innovative pricing model for mobile phones – or a dramatic anti-corruption campaign run by one of its tea-producing subsidiaries – Tata is full of innovators.

The innovation effort is led and guided from the top. Annual innovation awards recognize those who have come up with great ideas. Within these awards is a special category called 'Dare to Try'. Every year, three people are rewarded publicly for trying something that didn't actually work. We know it failed, the company says to them, but we really like the way you think. Keep going, and try again.

Passion for service, innovation, trust and reliability all lead to customer satisfaction. Tata comfortably outscores its rivals in satisfaction surveys, not just among customers but all stakeholders. As for financial performance, the Tata group worldwide now turns over more than $100 billion a year. If performance in some areas such as steel is rocky, performance in others such as cars and consultancy service has been stellar. The amount of money Tata Sons sends to its charitable shareholders has jumped many times over the past twenty years, meaning the shareholders are very well satisfied.

Satisfied employees, commitment to innovation, satisfied customers, profit. Of course, there is more to it than just putting these building blocks into place. The task of the leader is to put the process into motion, lining up the elements and guiding and focusing on the end goal. To see this is done, it is time to turn to the second half of the equation, the ethical value chain.

5

The Ethical Value Chain

The process of creating value through being ethical doesn't happen by itself. No alchemy is involved, no magic wands are waved, and, unless Hogwarts decides to open a business school, this isn't going to change. The process can be a long one and requires a considerable investment of time and effort.

There is some evidence that social media is beginning to have a positive impact. In February 2018 British Boxers, a Staffordshire-based company that makes underwear and nightwear and prides itself on its ethical employment and procurement policies, was approached by an advertising salesman from the *Daily Mail* and asked if it wished to place an ad. The response was thank you, but no. The news spread like wildfire across social media, and the company was suddenly deluged with orders from people wanting to support its policy. In a tweet, British Boxers said it had done more business in two days than it had in the week before Christmas.

BRITISH BOXERS @GrandpaJem

We've taken more sales in the last two days than we took in the week before Christmas just because we said 'No thank you' to advertising in The Mail and you lot retweeted us. YOU ARE AMAZING! That's your power. You did that. Thank you so, so much.

As Philip Crosby famously said, 'quality is free', meaning that the money you invest in quality management will be returned many times over in the form of better products, satisfied customers and higher profits.[1] The same is true of ethics. Once ethics is fully embedded in the business model and stakeholders begin to realize that you mean what our company means what it says and can be trusted, then the time and effort spent will yield loyal employees and customers, higher profits and, in turn, happy shareholders.

It is worth reiterating that ethical business is not just a matter of laying off risk, of avoiding the problems that have beset organizations like Uber and Oxfam and that brought down the Weinstein Company. As Aristotle said, not doing wrong because we are afraid of getting caught does not make us ethical. The real purpose of ethical business is to create value. That is why businesses exist; that is why the whole concept of business evolved in the first place, as a way of satisfying society's needs and wants. That brings us to the ethical value chain.

The concept of the value chain was popularized by Professor Michael Porter in the 1980s in his book *Competitive Advantage*, although contrary to popular belief, he did not invent the idea.[2] He did produce a very successful codification of the concept which is still widely used today. For the benefit of those who have not read *Competitive Advantage*, very briefly, Porter defines the value chain as a set of activities that a business performs in order to deliver products or service to the market. He divides these into five primary activities – inbound logistics, operations, outbound logistics, marketing and sales, and service – and four secondary activities – procurement, human resource management, technological development and infrastructure.

Value chain analysis involves looking at each of the activities in turn, describing what it is the firm currently does, and then analysing that activity to see what value it is adding and how. Areas of underperformance, where the activity is not adding enough value, can be highlighted and corrective measures taken.

The ethical value chain is a little different. Rather than considering different parts of the business model, it looks at generic activities that run *across* the business model and cover every function and activity. Also, the ethical value chain does not just consider value created for the company. It also considers value creation for all stakeholders, everyone who is affected by the company's operations in some way. The Tata Group's code of conduct lists the following stakeholders who are deemed to be of importance:

- Employees

- Customers

- Communities and the environment

- Value-chain partners including suppliers, service providers, distributors, sales representatives, contractors, consultants, intermediaries and agents

- Joint venture partners and other business associates

- Financial stakeholders

- Governments

- Individual companies within the Tata Group[3]

It is important to ensure that all stakeholders are treated with equal fairness. Just because we treat our customers well and ensure they are looked after does not mean we can mistreat our employees with impunity. Delta Airlines, once famous for its customer service, found this out the hard way when it cut its staff training budget and put a squeeze on wages. Delta staff had been famous for their smiles, but when the new measures came in, they stopped smiling. Customers noticed the staff were unhappy and grumpy, and switched to other airlines. Within a few years, Delta was filing for protection from bankruptcy.

There is also an argument for including competitors and rivals on this list. Of course we should compete hard, but we should also compete fairly. John

ESTABLISHING THE ETHICAL POSITION
↓
COMMUNICATING VALUES AND STANDARDS
↓
MOTIVATING OTHERS
↓
MONITORING ETHICAL PERFORMANCE
↓
ENSURING CONTINUITY

FIGURE 2 *The ethical value chain.*

Patterson, the man who turned National Cash Register (NCR) into a world-class company, was a caring and compassionate employer who looked after his workers. NCR was also famous for its high-quality customer service. When it came to rivals in the market, however, Patterson was ruthless, using any means, legal or illegal, to drive them out of the market. Eventually public opinion turned against Patterson and the US government authorities filed charges against him. NCR had to pay a very heavy fine and curtail its activities, and Patterson himself only escaped prison thanks to his extensive record as a philanthropist.

The key activities in the ethical code of conduct are laid out in Figure 1. Let us look at each of them in turn.

Establishing the ethical position

The organization needs to establish, as clearly and precisely as possible, what its values are, what it stands for and believes in, and what activities it is willing to tolerate and what is unacceptable. Deontologically, this means establishing principles of right and wrong, beginning with compliance with the law and any established industry codes of practice. Issues such as disrespectful behaviour towards other staff and customers, privacy and data safeguarding, conflict of interest and so on need also to be discussed and standards set.

These standards can be embedded in a code of conduct, or code of ethics, but ideally such a code should be much more than just a list of thou-shalt-nots. The Tata Code of Conduct sets out a number of positive core principles that reflect the Tata Group's mission, including points such as 'we seek to contribute to the economic development of the communities of the countries and regions we operate in', 'we shall act with professionalism, honesty and integrity, and conform to the highest moral and ethical standards', and 'we shall strive to balance the interests of our stakeholders, treating each of them fairly'.[4]

How formally these principles need to be laid out depends to a large extent on the size of the organization. If you are leading a small team or running a small business with a handful of people, there might be no need for a written document, provided everyone talks about and discusses ethical standards and is aware of what is required. In larger organizations, a written document is a good idea, as it gives everyone a single point of reference. A written document can also be useful for legal reasons should an ethical breach occur; it can be important to have evidence that everyone was aware of the ethical standards required and ignorance is no defence.

Next, the organization needs to take a consequentialist position and examine the value it creates for each of the stakeholder groups above. By value, we mean the utility or satisfaction that each stakeholder derives from their relationship with us. What do our employees gain? Wages, job satisfaction, skills, the society of other like-minded people? What do our customers gain? Useful goods and services that improve their well-being, or their self-esteem? What does the community as a whole gain? Prosperity, through job creation? Better standards of living through goods and services that improve lives? A general increase in happiness through consumption?

Answering these questions for each stakeholder group can be time-consuming. The law of unintended consequences needs to be considered: is the impact we are actually having on these groups the impact we intended? Economists talk about *externalities*, impacts of business activity that are felt by people who did not choose to pay for them. Negative or harmful externalities include things like passive smoking, or breathing air polluted with diesel fumes, or flood damage and erosion caused by deforestation. There can also be positive externalities, for example, breathing cleaner air as more electric vehicles come onto the market. From an ethical point of view, it is vitally important to consider all these externalities and make certain we are aware of them. Consultants such as environmental auditors can be useful to help the process go forward.

Once we are aware of the value and consequences of the activities of our business, we can look at the options for the business. Which will result in the maximum amount of good, and the minimum amount of harm? Which, if we prefer to adopt the utilitarian approach, will yield the greatest good for the greatest number? From an ethical perspective we need to consider how each option will affect *all* stakeholder groups, and not privilege one or two over the others. If even one stakeholder group is unhappy, that can damage the reputation of the business and make it harder to reach our goal.

Remember, too, the pragmatic position: the ends are inseparable from the means. Actions have consequences. *How* we do things is just as important as *what* we do, or what our objective is.

Finally, we need to consider virtue ethics. What kind of organization do we want to be? What kind of reputation do we want to have? What are the principle virtues – courage, generosity, truthfulness, compassion – that will be necessary to make this a truly ethical organization? How do we go about cultivating those in ourselves, and spreading them through the rest of the organization? If we can make our entire organization virtuous, then the need for a deontological code changes. It is still important to have the code, but now it becomes a reminder, a signpost to the way forward, rather than an instrument of control to restrain behaviour. The best codes of conduct are the ones people adhere to voluntarily, without the need for enforcement.

It is important that the process of establishing the ethical position involves as many people as possible from every stakeholder group. Leaders are responsible

---

ESTABLISHING THE POSITION

- Deontology: set the required standards and create a code of conduct
- Consequentialism: describe the value that the business creates and its impact on stakeholders, including externalities
- Pragmatism: remember the ends are inseparable from the means, and choose actions with positive consequences
- Virtue ethics: decide what kind of organization we want to be

---

for ensuring that the process takes place, that a position *is* established and that everyone has a voice. But for the leaders to decide unilaterally what is right and what is wrong, what is good and what is bad in terms of outcomes and consequences for every stakeholder group is dangerous. It would require someone with very formidable powers of empathy to put themselves into the minds of every single group and think like those stakeholders think. It is far easier and less risky to communicate with these other groups, listen to them and take their views on board, and then create a synthesis that will satisfy, if not everyone, then as many people as possible.

There may be some black-and-white issues where extensive consultation is not necessary. There can be no argument with laying down a rule that says staff will not give or receive bribes, not when such activity is clearly illegal. In many other cases there will be shades of grey. Rather than imposing our own ethical views and values on others, which itself has ethical implications, it is almost certainly better to find out what values others hold and then look for common ground.

MONDRAGÓN CORPORATION

In 1943, a priest named José Maria Arizmendiarrieta founded a technical college in the Spanish town of Mondragón in an effort to restore prosperity to the impoverished Basque region. In 1956 the college spun off a small co-operative business called Ulgor. More co-operatives followed over the years, and at time of writing more than a hundred co-operatively owned businesses exist as part of the Mondragón Corporation. Mondragón operates internationally, and in 2017 posted revenues of around €13 billion, making it one of Spain's largest business groups.

Mondragón's founding ethos was one of co-operation and collaboration, communities pulling together in the face of adversity to work for mutual prosperity and become self-sufficient. The business has remained remarkably robust, despite the bankruptcy and sale of one of its largest members, domestic appliance maker Fagor, in 2013. The rest of the group survived the sharp economic downturn in Spain post-2008, and in part thanks to its efforts, the Basque region remains one of the most prosperous parts of Spain.

Mondragón has an established set of values and principles which are reviewed and updated regularly, but remain consistent with the group's founding ethos of co-operation and spreading wealth through the community. Its current code of values includes the following key points, all embedded in its founding principles:

- Democratic organization
- Sovereignty of labour
- The instrumental and subordinate nature of capital
- Participatory management
- Inter-cooperation between the firms within the group
- Social transformation
- Education[5]

Communicating values and standards

'Spreading virtues through the organization'? Easy enough, perhaps, if you are leading a team of five or six, where you know everyone personally. You can talk to people face to face, see their reactions, engage in discussions and give-and-take. If you are leading an organization of hundreds of thousands dispersed around the world, not so much. The patience of Mother Teresa and the strength of Hercules will be required (or, perhaps, the other way around).

Getting the message across is not just a matter of speaking the words. People have to believe you really mean it, that you really are communicating a deeply felt and believed set of ethical values, and not preaching one message while practicing something quite different. Before they will believe you, they must first trust you, and that is why ethical leaders talk so much about leading by example.

Leading by example

As we saw above, the first step in persuading others to be ethical is to behave in an ethical manner yourself. Senior leaders at Tata talk a great deal about walking the walk, or, sometimes, confusingly, 'walking the talk'. (Both mean the same thing; just remember to nod approvingly if you hear either one, and do not under any circumstances be tempted to get into a discussion about which is correct. Tata managers love abstruse philosophical discussions. You will be there for days.) Ratan Tata, when he was chairman of the group, set great store by this, putting his own ethical beliefs into practice and living his professional and personal life in a manner in keeping with his deeply held values. His management team took their cue from him, their own followers from them, and so on down through hierarchy.

Most of us, when we see people behaving ethically, admire them for doing so. We feel drawn to them, and if we are part of the same organization, we will tend to support them and draw closer to them. We also tend, even if only subconsciously, to model our behaviour on theirs. Michael Brown and colleagues see this as a form of social learning.[6] Rather, as children mimic the habits of their parents, we adapt our own style and ways of doing things to those of leaders we respect and admire. If a respected and admired leader behaves in an ethical manner, it is much more likely that the rest of the organization will behave ethically as well.

Of course, leading by example on its own is not sufficient. People have to see you and be aware of your example, for a start, and so communication and relationship-building skills are also vitally important. But these in turn are of very little value unless we ourselves are considered trustworthy individuals whose message should be believed. Vitally important is the concept of authenticity, discussed by writers such as Inma Adarves-Yorno and Herminia Ibarra.[7] For those not familiar with the term, authenticity simply means being genuine and communicating who you really are, rather than trying to pretend to be something you are not. Authenticity, living according to your own values, is closely tied to ethical behaviour.

This may sound more complicated than it really is. A lot of leading by example comes back the Aristotelian virtues, generosity, kindness, empathy for others. Mother Teresa, whom we mentioned above, had a saying: 'be faithful in the small things, for it is in them that your strength lies.' I have found that saying 'thank you' to people in a professional context is extremely powerful. People remember you for thanking them; they feel they can trust you, oxytocin is released and they feel happy. (Giving them chocolate would probably have the same effect.) A colleague, a consultant who works with small businesses, says that smiling and saying hello to the receptionist when you walk through the front door also has a very strong effect. Receptionists know everyone, and word quickly gets around.

It should be added too that authenticity and leading by example are equally important when dealing with *all* stakeholders, inside and outside the organization. I have been particularly impressed by how Paul Polman presents a very consistent image and message no matter whether he is talking to employees, customers and shareholders. Through both his words and actions, he communicates the ethical values he is enshrining at Unilever, and all stakeholders are aware of his intentions. As Mary Jo Hatch and Majken Schultz point out in their book *Taking Brand Initiative*, consistency of message is extremely important across all forms of communication. Each stakeholder must receive the same message, even if it is couched in different terms. Once different stakeholder groups start receiving different messages, the image and values begin to become blurred, and this will in time affect and erode trust.[8]

Promulgating the code of conduct

Communicating the code of conduct is important too, and this too can serve as a signpost to external stakeholders as well as staff. Letting people know what you stand for, what you believe to be right and wrong, is important. It sets expectations.

Promulgating the entire code of conduct is not always practical. Some codes of conduct run to many pages and includes examples of desired and prohibited behaviours, frequently asked questions and much else besides. But condensed versions of the ethics and values can be used as part of external branding. McKinsey's values are frequently shared with clients in an effort to make it clear what McKinsey believes about itself and the standards it will try to uphold during a client engagement.

Talking and listening

Communicating ethical values and principles should take the form of a dialogue. An 'I talk, you listen' approach is unlikely to generate much enthusiasm. At worst, it could be seen as an attempt by leadership to push their own values and beliefs onto the followers without consent, and then expect the followers to perform. This can breed resentment and passive resistance.

As leaders, we need to remember that it is not just our ethics that matter. Stakeholders have their own ethical codes and beliefs too. We might disagree with what they consider to be ethical, we might even in some cases find their beliefs repugnant, but we have no right to ram our views down their throats at gunpoint.

Instead, we lay out our position and argue our case logically, with dignity and respect for opposing points of view. When persuading others to recognize and follow our ethical business approach, we need to explain why are adopting this approach, and what benefits it will bring in terms of reputation, trust, profits and so on according to the value creation model in the previous chapter. We need to explain what is in it for them. Again, that includes shareholders, customers and suppliers as well as employees.

The Eden Project in Cornwall sets high standards for its suppliers and expects them to conform to fair trade standards. However, rather than kicking out suppliers who fall short of those standards, Eden works with them to help them raise their game.[9] In China, following an incident in 2008 when infant milk formula was contaminated with melamine, resulting in six deaths and tens of thousands of illnesses, Tetra Pak stepped in to work with partners up and down the milk value chain to help them improve their hygiene standards and product safety. In most cases Tetra Pak provided consultancy advice, training and even equipment for free.[10] Sometimes, the best and most effective form of communication is action.

I have described leading by example, promulgating codes of values and dialogue through talking and listening as if they were sequential steps, but clearly they are not. All four needed to be done simultaneously, and what is

COMMUNICATING VALUES AND STANDARDS

- Deontology: communicate the required standards and code of conduct
- Consequentialism: explain and discuss the value being created and the consequences of business activity
- Pragmatism: build multiple relationships with different stakeholders to hear diverse points of view
- Virtue ethics: be the kind of person you want to be, and encourage others to do the same

more, they need to be done all the time. The ethical leader will find that doing these things takes up a significant portion of his or her time, every day. And so it should. To repeat another point made earlier in this book, leaders don't do things alone. They need their team, their organization, to make the journey with them.

I once interviewed a CEO who told me that communicating the organization's values was half his job. In my view, this is one of the reasons why CEOs exist; to help the organization recognize where it wants to go, and then assist it to get there by keeping it on course, part shepherd and part helmsman.

MCKINSEY

Like Mondragón, McKinsey & Company has a very strong set of values, many of which were established by the long-serving managing partner and architect of the firm in its modern form, Marvin Bower. The values are:

Adhere to the highest professional standards
- put client interests ahead of the firm's
- observe high ethical standards
- preserve client confidences
- maintain an independent perspective
- manage client and firm resources cost-effectively

Improve our clients' performance significantly
- follow the top-management approach
- use our global network to deliver the best of the firm to all clients
- bring innovations in management practice to clients
- build client capabilities to sustain improvement
- build enduring relationships based on trust

Create an unrivaled environment for exceptional people
- be nonhierarchical and inclusive
- sustain a caring meritocracy
- develop one another through apprenticeship and mentoring
- uphold the obligation to dissent
- govern ourselves as a 'one firm' partnership[11]

McKinsey communicates these values relentlessly to its own people and to its clients. Version of the values statement can be found in the reception area of every McKinsey office in the world, and are plastered across its websites and official communications. The firm holds annual 'values days' where staff get together and discuss the firm's values and what more can be done to uphold them.

The values statement are also a powerful part of the firm's marketing effort and lie at the core of its image and reputation with external stakeholders. Directors of McKinsey also regard themselves as values ambassadors, and one of their primary roles is to communicate the values to staff and customers, and ensure that the former adhere to the values. Failing to live up to the values, especially where client relationships are concerned, is one of the most heinous crimes a McKinsey staffer can commit, and partners have been terminated without notice for doing so.

Motivating others

Motivating others to behave ethically can be a simple matter of deontological compliance: behave ethically and we will reward you, fail and you will be punished. This is the approach followed by many organizations, and it is useful provided both reward and punishment are carried out in a fair and equitable manner. If not, then as Rawls's theory of justice suggests, there are obvious ethical implications.

However, there are other ways of thinking about motivation. Carrots are usually more effective than sticks. Work-based theories of motivation such as Herzberg's hygiene theory and Hackman and Oldham's job characteristics theory suggest that while employees are motivated by reward – pay and other monetary incentives, training opportunities, the chance for advancement – they are also strongly motivated by finding satisfaction in their work and knowing that their work has meaning for other people.[12]

This is particularly true of more highly skilled employees, as Rob Goffee and Gareth Jones point out in their *Harvard Business Review* article 'Leading Clever People'.[13] These people tend to be attracted to their professions in the first place, not just for the money but also for the chance to create something that will make an impact on the world around them. They set their own goals, and measure their own progress towards those goals, continuing to do so whatever further goals or restrictions we might impose on them.[14] Giving these people the space to create is one of the most powerful motivators around, and surveys have shown that this group will often voluntarily work for less money if they can find the right supportive environment.

This should be very helpful to the ethical leader, whose task is to persuade people to behave ethically. We have already established that creating value for other people lies at the heart of ethical leadership. Helping people to see the good their work is doing and giving them a space where they can go on to innovate and create further value will chime with the ambitions of many employees. And, considering the virtue ethics line, if we give them scope to develop their own virtues, this too should resonate.

Develop their own virtues? Oh, that really does sound a bit snowflakey, doesn't it? Come on, we're being far too soft. All we have to do is pay people well, and in return, when we say jump, they're supposed to ask how high

No. It doesn't work that way, and it never really has. There are a few people who doubtless only turn up to work because they know they're going to get paid, do the minimum amount and then go home when the job is done (and do you really want those people in your organization? Would you willingly hire them? And if so, why?), but there are many more who are looking for something that will give their lives meaning and purpose; and for someone who can help them find it. Mary Parker Follett, speaking at a Rowntree Management Conference in 1928, summed up that yearning:

I believe that the great leader can … arouse my latent possibilities, can reveal to me new powers in myself, can quicken and give direction to some force within me. There is energy, passion, unawakened life in us – those who call it forth are our leaders.[15]

Public recognition can be a form of reward, depending on the company and its culture. Not everyone welcomes public attention. Some love to be recognized in public; others would rather walk barefoot over hot coals than stand up on stage and receive an award. Sometimes a simple handshake and a quiet 'well done' will be just as effective at recognizing behaviour and building an ongoing relationship.

Other stakeholders will have their own needs, but we can find ways of rewarding them too. Shareholders want money, but they also want reassurance that the company is being well managed; and increasingly, many shareholders are also concerned that the companies they invest in are ethically managed. Suppliers like steady relationships, and, as we saw above, they are often happy to receive technical help and support to improve their own businesses. Customers want value for money, but they are also impressed by simple kindness.

My wife once pointed out to our local supermarket that they had charged her for a dozen bottles of cleaning fluid instead of a dozen bottles of wine, a discrepancy of nearly a hundred pounds. In thanks, the supermarket gave her a bouquet of flowers and box of chocolates. There it is, chocolate again. It may be the answer to all our problems.

MOTIVATING OTHERS

- Deontology: punishing unethical behaviour and rewarding those who meet or exceed ethical standards
- Consequentialism: helping other people to do good
- Pragmatism: giving people the scope to create and innovate
- Virtue ethics: giving people the scope to develop their own virtue and become the people they want to be

JOHN LEWIS

The John Lewis Partnership motivates its employees by involving them not just in ownership but in the management of the business. As John Lewis himself said, mere ownership is not enough. Employees must also have power and control over what they own, in order to make that ownership meaningful. Each employee is a partner in the organization, and, in the John Lewis group's own communications, the word 'employee' is not used; people are referred to instead as 'partners'.

The governing body of the John Lewis Partnership is the Partnership Council, composed of eighty-two members. Eighty per cent of these are elected by the 85,000 partners, with the chairman appointing the remainder. The two principal businesses in the group, department store chain John Lewis and Waitrose supermarkets, each have their own council with a similar composition. These councils have the power to discuss any matter concerning the business, and function in effect as non-executive directors, overseeing and scrutinizing what the executives do and holding them to account.[16]

Each individual store also has a branch forum where partners can meet and discuss issues. These forums are strong sources for innovation. Partners can and do suggest ways of improving customer service which are forwarded to management either directly or through the Partnership Council. The combination of ownership and the power to create change motivates employees to take a greater interest in the organization and to drive the quest for greater value.

So strong is this motivation that the Partnership Council has resisted all attempts to break the partnership. In 1999, following a run of poor results, it was proposed that the company should be sold. This would have netted each partner around £100,000. Instead, the Partnership Council vowed to work to improve the company and turn around its fortunes. Only one member of the Partnership Council voted in favour of a sale.[17]

Monitoring ethical performance

This is a slightly tricky issue because monitoring people itself has ethical implications. Monitoring and measuring progress can be used as means of sanctioning or disciplining people by setting targets they cannot reach and then punishing them for their failure. This was one of the arguments against scientific management and pay-for-performance cultures. It is all very well to reward people for their efforts, but punishing them for failure can be done only if strict principles of justice and fairness are adhered to.

Even then, the consequences can be unpleasant. If people know they could be punished, their behaviour may become more risk-averse as they seek to avoid any action or behaviour that might make them culpable. How many times have you asked an organization for information, only to be told that information is not available on the grounds of 'data protection'? In my experience, in the majority of such cases, giving the information would not breach data protection rules. But staff, unsure of what the regulations actually say, would rather refuse to give out data than risk falling foul of the law.

W. Edwards Deming, the late twentieth-century quality guru and one of the founders of total quality management, once argued that all targets, quotas and statistical goals should be abolished.[18] This is a radical idea (and, for some, a quite terrifying one). I agree with Deming that the idea of setting numerical targets raises many ethical questions. For the ethical leader, it can be very useful to set standards and ask people to adhere to them, but, as I have argued above, that alone is not enough. Ethical performance should be voluntary, and monitoring should be a matter of (a) getting an overall feeling for whether the business is moving towards its goals and creating a maximum of value with a minimum of externalities, and (b) whether any individuals are, through either error or deliberate action, behaving in an unethical manner.

As we said, people in businesses make mistakes. In terms of monitoring performance, one of the tasks of the ethical leader is to step in and ensure that failures are dealt with quickly and responsibly. Once again, the ethical thing to do also turns out to be the right thing to do from the perspective of the business.

MONITORING ETHICAL PERFORMANCE

- Deontology: setting targets for ethical actions and measuring them
- Consequentialism: setting targets for value creation and measuring them
- Pragmatism: allowing people to set their own targets; light-touch monitoring to ensure there are no breaches
- Virtue ethics: creating an environment in which ethical decisions are made automatically, with no need to monitor

---

We saw in Chapter 1 how Facebook delayed its response to the revelations about Cambridge Analytica and consequently took a big hit to its reputation, whereas Cricket Australia reacted quickly to the ball-tampering scandal and was able to salvage something from the wreckage. Speed of response is important, but so too is a display of virtue. When business failures happen, it is important to respond with kindness and compassion.

Two more examples of failure will help to reinforce the point. The first is oil giant BP's reaction to the *Deepwater Horizon* disaster, in which an oil exploded and caught fire, killing eleven people and causing an oil spill that affected large parts of the Gulf of Mexico. CEO Tony Hayward was widely criticized for not taking the event seriously enough at first, downplaying the level of pollution and insisting the spill was not a serious event. 'We made a few little mistakes early on', he told reporters.[19] Although he later changed his position and apologized for the spill, the damage was done and Hayward had effectively forfeited the trust of the public. He resigned three months later.

The second example concerns the Malaysia Airlines flight MH370, which disappeared on a flight from Malaysia to China in 2014 and has never been found. None of the authorities connected with this tragedy comes out of it particularly well, with the Malaysian government releasing conflicting stories and information, but Malaysia Airlines came in for particular criticism when it sent out a bluntly worded, unsympathetic text to the families of the victims:

Malaysia Airlines deeply regrets that we have to assume beyond any reasonable doubt that MH370 has been lost and that none of those on board has survived. As you will hear in the next hour from Malaysia's Prime Minister, we must now accept all evidence suggests the plane went down in the southern Indian Ocean.[20]

Many of the family members were angry and horrified and the airline was roundly criticized for its lack of sympathy. Lack of compassion on the part of managers was one factor in the subsequent collapse of the airline's share price and, ultimately, its failure.

Contrast this with the behaviour of Air France following the crash of Flight 447 on its way from Rio de Janeiro to Paris in 2009. Within an hour of the plane's disappearance off radar screens, senior Air France executives, including its chairman, were with relatives waiting at Charles de Gaulle airport, speaking to them, giving them whatever information they had, comforting them and offering sympathy. Air France's executives did everything they could to ease the suffering of the grieving people, and the company was widely praised as a result. Its share price dipped briefly after the accident, but recovered its full value within a week.

Maple Leaf Foods: The public interest

On 12 August 2008 the management of food processing company Maple Leaf Foods became aware of a possible case of listeriosis contamination at one of its meat processing plants near Toronto. By 23 August the contamination had been confirmed, and by the end of September 2008 twenty-one deaths had been linked to the listeriosis outbreak. Many more people fell ill.

Faced with a disaster that could have broken the business as well as affecting many lives, Maple Leaf Foods took prompt action. CEO Michael McCain led from the front, offering an immediate apology to everyone affected and taking full responsibility. Instead of just recalling the product lines contaminated by listeria, the company pulled every single line from all of its plants, and resumed production only when tests showed the production lines were clear of contamination. 'The core principle is to do what is in the interest of public health', McCain said.

As well as holding frequent news conferences to keep the press updated, Maple Leaf Foods used its website to provide information about the steps it was taking to eliminate further contamination. This website was updated on a round-the-clock basis, seven days a week. The company also produced a television advertisement making a further apology and explaining the company's response. Although the financial impacts were severe, Maple Leaf Foods returned to profitability a year later and regained most of the business it had lost following the crisis.[21]

Tata Finance: Saying it from the heart

Resolving failures takes courage, and it is here that some organizations and some leaders fail to the test. The temptation to blame someone else, to run and hide until it all blows over, can be very strong. One of the true tests of an ethical leader is how they meet the challenge of failure. Michael McCain met that challenge head on. So too did Ratan Tata when, in 2002, it became apparent that the group's financial services company, Tata Finance, had run into trouble.

The first sign that all was not well came when the auditors refused to sign off on Tata Finance's books. The auditing firm fired the auditors and brought in others who agreed to sign off. At this point alarm bells began to ring at Bombay House, the group's headquarters, and an internal review began. It was quickly discovered that there was a black hole of unknown size in Tata Finance's accounts.

'We could have plugged the hole quietly and made good the losses' Ratan Tata told me several years later. 'But I could not do that. We would have been allowing the guilty to walk away. I felt that if we did not make this public, then we were implicitly saying that this sort of behaviour was tolerable.'[22] Tata in effect blew the whistle on itself and reported the matter to the regulators, and several executives of Tata Finance were arrested. Ratan Tata then took an action which, so far as I know, is unprecedented in the history of banking. Even though the size of the black hole was still unknown, he promised to reimburse every customer of Tata Finance who had lost money, down to the last rupee.

He didn't have to do this. As R. Gopalakrishnan, executive director of Tata Sons, pointed out, Tata Finance was a limited liability company; it could have simply walked away and left its customers to fend for themselves, as so many other failed banks have done over the years. 'But he promised we would cover all the losses, even though we did not know what they were', Gopalakrishnan told me. 'He was really saying it from the heart.' Ratan Tata himself believes he had no real choice. 'If we had not done this, then no one would ever have trusted us again', he said. 'And everything we had worked for would have been thrown away.'[23]

I referred earlier in the book to Ajit Nayak's article, 'Wisdom and the Tragic Question'. This is what Ajit means by wisdom: knowing what is right, and having the courage to do it. And, most of the time, if you do what is right, people will respect you for it and trust you, and the damage can be limited.

The *Deepwater Horizon* explosion, the loss of MH370, these were not *ethical* failures. They were failures pure and simple, accidents that could happen anytime to anyone. True. But the response to failure *does* have an ethical dimension. How we take responsibility, how we move to help those with whom we have relationships and to whom we are responsible, will be guided by our own ethical standards. We can run and hide, and shirk responsibility, or we can stand up, be accountable and do what is right. It is our choice.

SEMCO

At Semco, the Brazilian light engineering firm mentioned in Chapter 2, every employee takes responsibility for their own actions. No one monitors performance by individuals, only overall performance towards the objectives of the business plan. If this looks like falling short, employees put their heads together and work out how to get things back on track.

Can this be done with ethics? Can we really rely on people to be ethical, so we don't have to check on them? Once again, in small teams or organizations, this may be possible. If the leader successfully creates the ethical climate and everyone shares the same values and ethical beliefs, then it probably is. People can be expected to police themselves, and, if an ethical breach does occur, to put their hands up, admit it and then rectify the situation.

In larger organizations, this simply isn't possible. Human beings are fallible; they make mistakes, or succumb to temptation. Even highly values-driven organizations like Unilever and McKinsey, who have strong ethical codes and highly ethical cultures, have lapses. When that happens, someone has to step in and take responsibility for putting the situation right – and, if necessary, disciplining the people responsible for the lapse. In a perfect world, there would be no need for compliance officers. Sadly, the world is not perfect.

That does not mean, however, that we should not try to encourage people to be responsible for their own ethical behaviour. Even if we don't get as far down the road as Semco, some self-policing is still better than none.

Ensuring continuity

The final element in the ethical value chain is ensuring continuity. It is not enough to be ethical once. We have to keep doing it, day in and day out, week in and week out, year in and year out, walking the walk.

That does not mean doing the same thing over and over. Deming once wrote that quality is a journey, and ethics is much the same. No matter how ethical we and our organizations may be, we must keep raising the bar.

Kaizen, or continuous improvement, is a concept in quality management that favours constant, evolutionary change, making small adjustments as often as possible with the goal of constantly improving quality. Among its key principles are (1) feedback and reflection to examine what we are doing now and how we could do it better, and (2) encouraging people to take ownership of problems and work out solutions rather than waiting for someone else to do it.

We can apply the concepts of *kaizen* to ethical leadership. We must be constantly self-reflective, thinking about the decisions we have made and actions we have taken, examining the consequences and thinking what we will do differently – and better – next time. We must also be listeners, hearing feedback from others, not just our close colleagues but all our stakeholders. And we must encourage everyone we work with, especially our staff, to step up and take responsibility. One of the tasks of the ethical leader is to make it clear that ethics is everyone's responsibility. If we can do this, steadily over the long term, then we will gradually build trust and reputation and the self-fulfilling process we described in Chapter 4 will begin.

ENSURING CONTINUITY

Deontology: continuous monitoring of ethical performance for compliance with standards of right and wrong

Consequentialism: continuous improvement, raising the bar for value creation and challenging the organization to do more

Pragmatism: looking for new and different ways to create value across a spectrum of activities

Virtue ethics: developing people's ethical capacity to its fullest extent

TATA

Tata has been remarkably consistent in maintaining its ethical standards. There have been lapses of course, and the case of Tata Finance (above) is a particularly serious one. But on the whole, Tata has remained not only a scandal-free organization, but one that is widely admired for its very strong ethical stance. As discussed in the previous chapter, that stance plays an important role in value creation and is a cornerstone of the brand value.

Tata ensures consistency in three ways. The first is through the code of conduct, which every member of every Tata company reads and agrees to adhere to the day they join. The second is through leadership by example and constant communication of the company's ethical standards and values in the manner described in this chapter.

The third way is through constant reference to its past. Like McKinsey, another organization whose values are deeply rooted in its heritage, Tata harks back to the past and reminds its stakeholders of the great figures who created and upheld its ethics and values. The founder, Jamsetji Nusserwanji Tata, and his descendant and long-serving chairman in the twentieth century, J.R.D. Tata, are omnipresent figures in Tata folklore. Their portraits and busts are in every important public space in the company's offices and reception areas, visible and constant reminders. Their words and sayings are quoted in annual reports and other official communications.

Tata has been around for a hundred and fifty years, McKinsey is getting close to its century. Not every organization has these decades of tradition as a wellspring to draw on, but even relatively young organizations can hark back to their foundation and remember their original purpose and why they were created. Very few businesses are founded purely as a vehicle to make money. Most of the great corporations of today had a social purpose. Here are a few examples:

- Heinz: to make nourishing and sustainable food available to the people
- Kellogg's: to offer a healthy eating alternative at breakfast
- Coca-Cola: to offer a nourishing and stimulating drink that would be an alternative to alcoholic beverages

- Sony: to help rebuild the war-ravaged economy of Japan and create cheap, easy-to-use consumer goods
- IBM: to provide machines that would enable businesses to function more efficiently and serve customers more effectively

Referring to that core purpose can be a source of inspiration and help guide ethical thinking now and in future. Once again, it is about remembering what value you are creating and why, not getting hung up on short-term notions like profit.

Summing up

The five elements of the ethical value chain – establishing the ethical position, communicating values and standards, motivating others, monitoring ethical performance and ensuring continuity – are the engine room that powers the value creation process. If done well, these things will establish reputation and trust. Establishing the ethical position sets expectations; it tells the world what our organization aspires to, what its purpose is and what standards it sets for itself. Those aspirations and purpose and standards then need to be communicated so that everyone, inside and outside the organization, understands them clearly and knows who we are and what we believe in.

It is not enough to just communicate; we must also motivate and bring others along with us on the journey. We talked about authenticity in leadership, but often ethical leadership means encouraging others to be authentic too. We need to give people space to fulfil their own aspirations, while at the same time guiding and encouraging them to work for the good of the group and create value for stakeholders. If we can align those two things, personal aspiration and the good of the group, that is when the real value creation begins.

Nor, once having set the wheels in motion, can we step back and let the process run itself. Being an ethical leader means constantly watching, listening, monitoring, looking out for signs of failure and stepping in quickly when they occur, driving the process onward and ensuring that the quest for ethical behaviour and value creation is a never-ending one. No matter how 'good' we think we are, there will always be ethical failures and dilemmas and paradoxes that need to be dealt with. The ethical leader must chart the organization's way past these, navigating through the obstacles and seeking clear water.

How do we do this on a daily basis? Wisdom and courage, virtue and common sense are all required, but there are also some tools and frameworks that can guide our thinking when making ethical decisions, and we will come back to these at the end of the book. First, it would be useful to explore the relationship between some of the key groups' stakeholders and the value chain in a little more detail. We will look at four groups – employees, customers, community, shareholders – in turn.

6

The Source of Our Prosperity: Employees

Conventional stakeholder theory, heavily rooted in John Rawls's theory of justice, argues that all who have a relationship with an organization, or who are affected by its actions, have a 'stake' or a vested interest in what that organization does.[1] It follows that all stakeholders should be treated equally, or, at least, that their interests should be regarded as being of equal importance.

True, but as we saw above in Chapter 4, there is a strong case for employees to be treated as *primus inter pares*. Without hard-working, dedicated employees, not much will get done and the organization has very little chance of reaching its goals. And, of course, there is the argument that if you look after your employees, they will look after your customers for you.

As employers, we have a duty of care towards our employees and we should look after them and their well-being. As Robert Owen and Edward Cadbury and many others since have learned, this is partly a matter of enlightened self-interest. Fear, stress, fatigue and unsafe working conditions all have a negative impact on productivity. Yet, it seems, there are many employers who refuse to see this, and believe that good management equates to exploiting employees as ruthlessly as possible in the pursuit of short-term gain.

Most of us will have experienced this at first hand. As a young man working my way through university in Canada I undertook a variety of jobs, perhaps the least salubrious of which was working as dishwasher on the midnight shift at a twenty-four-hour pancake house. On one occasion, running a fever and clearly suffering from flu, I called in sick, only to be told that 'we don't allow that sort of thing here', and that if I wanted to keep my job I had better turn up for work. Ordering employees suffering from a contagious illness to work an environment where food, or at least something resembling food, was being prepared for public consumption was not an intelligent thing to do, on either a moral or a practical level.

Yet it still goes on. Sports Direct is also alleged to have fired workers for calling in sick, and the same allegation has been made about other firms as well. Back in the 1920s, Seebohm Rowntree and his colleagues at the Rowntree conferences urged management and labour to realize that they were on the same side, but the notion that the employer–employee relationship is primarily an adversarial one is taking a long time to die. Uber's culture of 'principled confrontation' turned out on closer inspection to just be 'confrontation'.

A large part of the problem lies in a managerial attitude that persists in seeing staff as a resource, or, even worse, as cost centres. 'There's no point in trying to increase sales', a finance director (who shall remain nameless) recently told me. 'It's risky and difficult, and you never make as much money as you think you will. If you want to improve your margins, it's far better to make cuts. Cuts are easy.'

But Rowntree was right, and so were John Lewis and Ricardo Semler. The people who create value for the firm and for all its stakeholders are the workers. Management and workers are partners in the task of value creation. Within that partnership, the role of management is to support and enable the workers, so that they create more value, more efficiently and more effectively. If managers fail to do so, then it is they who are the cost centres.

Leading people ethically

Theories of ethical leadership of people and organizations usually start with a deontological perspective. Going back to the value chain, we establish the ethical position. We make rules about what is and is not acceptable; we promulgate codes of conduct; we communicate the message and establish an ethically minded culture. We establish norms for equity and fairness. How formal these are depends on the organization, its size and its culture, but the basic principle will still be the same. Even unwritten rules are still rules.

In practice, establishing the position includes issues such as equal pay for equal work, equal opportunities for advancement and promotion, transparency of information and so on. It also means establishing mechanisms for compliance, along with penalties for non-compliance.

There is also a consequentialist element. When we communicate the norms and values – the second stage in the value chain – we also point out the benefits to the organization. We appeal to enlightened self-interest. Being ethical will build reputation and gain the trust of other stakeholders, making the organization itself stronger and more resilient, and more profitable. We want our employees to behave ethically because we hope this will lead to a good outcome.

This is the standard approach to ethical leadership, but we can go much further. Promulgating codes of conduct and communicating values is essentially defensive, the equivalent of putting on a suit of armour. Google's famous motto, 'do no evil', tells people what not to do, but it doesn't tell them what they can do. Ethical leadership does more than just put up fences. It also opens gates.

The pragmatic approach to ethics argues that for every situation there are multiple options. Applying pragmatism to leadership means encouraging people to try different things, invent and innovate. Tata's 'Dare to Try' awards are an example of this. In order to foster such a culture, we need to take away barriers, physical and psychological, and ensure that people feel free to create. As Amantha Imber pointed out in a recent article in *Harvard Business Review*, this can also involve a degree of challenge. 'When thinking about goals you want to work towards', she says, 'make sure that there is at least one in the mix that gets you out of your comfort zone and pushes you enough to make you unsure whether you can achieve it.'[2]

Of course there is a risk here. If people become too fixed on goals, they may be tempted to take shortcuts to achieve them. There is a tricky balance to be found between deontological restriction and pragmatic motivation to innovate and succeed. Rather than relying too heavily on rule, we should look instead at *how* we motivate people, and how we encourage them to develop their own standards of behaviour and action rather than relying on those we impose upon them.

Herbert Kelman's work on attitude change can be useful here. Kelman, who worked on how attitudes change during conflict and stress, identified three ways that attitudes can change:

- Compliance: we obey orders given to us by others, though internally, our attitudes may not necessarily change. For example, a soldier obeys and order given by a superior officer, even though he or she might not agree with the order.

- Identification: in group situations, we change our views to match those of the majority around us in order to fit in. This might be a genuine attitude change, or it might be a chameleon move in order to make us less conspicuous or avoid conflict with the rest of the group. To continue with the example of the soldier, he or she wants to be part of the unit and share in its camaraderie, so modifies his or her attitudes to match those of the group.

- Internalization: we are persuaded by argument or example and shift our own views internally to adopt new attitudes and beliefs. No compulsion or coercion is involved; the change is entirely voluntary.[3]

In this case, the soldier buys into the culture and norms of the group and genuinely adopts them as his or her own. This soldier will obey orders without question; even more, he or she will often know what to do without needing orders at all.

Kelman was quite clear that compliance is the least effective method of changing attitudes, and internalization is the most effective, with identification somewhere in between. Compliance and identification are less deep-rooted and more prone to roll-back if things change, but employees who identify with the group are much more likely to remain loyal. With the first two, there is a strong need to monitor compliance and ensure continuity, the final two stages of the value chain.

However, if employees identify personally with the ethical standards and internalize them, they will very often police themselves. Monitoring and continuity become light-touch activities.

ESTABLISHING THE ETHICAL POSITION

Employment policies, equity and fairness, trust

COMMUNICATING VALUES AND STANDARDS

Talking to people, communicating the vision, leadership by example, authenticity

MOTIVATING OTHERS

Seeking commitment through identification and internalization

MONITORING ETHICAL PERFORMANCE

Looking out for exceptions, encouraging people to police themselves

ENSURING CONTINUITY

Upholding the ethical position, ensuring standards to not slip

---

FIGURE 3 *The ethical value chain: employees.*

Virtue and authenticity

Virtue ethics, as we have seen, involves looking into ourselves and deciding what kind of person we want to be. We behave virtuously not because we are frightened of the consequences if we do not, but because we know it is the right thing to do.

We can apply the same principle to organizations. A virtuous organization is one where all employees share a common set of values and have internalized them, so that everyone knows what needs to be done. Once again, though, it is easy to do this in small organizations, where the leader knows everyone and everyone knows the leader. How can we create this kind of culture in an organization employing hundreds of thousands scattered around the world?

Part of the answer lies in recruitment, picking people who are predisposed to fit with the organizational culture we want to create, and part lies in training and induction. Earlier, too, we discussed authenticity and walking the walk. It is vitally important the leader leads by example. In Kelner's model, the boundary between identification and internalization is porous; if we model our beliefs and actions on those of other people we respect and admire, over time we come to adopt those beliefs and actions as our own.

But it is not just leaders who need to be authentic. Followers also crave authenticity, the chance to be themselves rather than just cogs in a corporate machine. In a Harvard Business School working paper, David Sirota and his colleagues point out that highly motivated people have three goals at work:

- Equity: to be respected and treated fairly;

- Achievement: to be proud of their job, their achievements and their employer;

- Camaraderie: to have good productive relationships with their fellow employees.[4]

One of the tasks of the ethical leader is to ensure that employees get what they want from their work. If they do, then they will become effectively both self-leading and self-policing where ethics are concerned. After a while, like Semler and John Lewis, the leader may find himself or herself looking into the mirror and wondering if they are still really necessary. In another *Harvard Business Review* article, Rob Goffee and Gareth Jones asked the question: how do you lead clever people? Although Goffee and Jones give various tips for managing workplaces full of clever people, the answer to the question in the end is very simple: you don't. You give them a space where they can lead themselves, and let them get on with it.

Carl Zeiss Jena

The optical equipment maker Carl Zeiss Jena was founded in the south German city of Jena in 1846. The company operated on a fairly small scale for many years, making precision instruments such as microscopes, but the business really took off when Carl Zeiss, the founder, recruited a 26-year-old professor of physics at the University of Jena, Ernst Abbé, initially as a director of research. Abbé quickly became a full partner in the business and then took over as managing director after Zeiss's death in 1888. The company grew rapidly and developed an international reputation as the world's leading instrument maker. By 1900 it employed 1,400 people and had a turnover of around £1 million.

Abbé had no formal training as a manager or business leader, but he had a genuine passion for innovation, and ensured that this same passion was diffused throughout the firm. He gave his scientific and technical staff an entirely free hand. Their primary role was to do research and create knowledge. Once that was done, the results of their experiments were examined to see if they had commercial potential. If they did not, the researcher either proceeded to the next stage of the research or abandoned the project and picked up something new. What they did was entirely up to them, and Abbé backed his researchers even if it took them years to produce a viable product. But Abbé did not merely sit back and watch his workers. He took a close interest in their work, and challenged them to be innovative and to succeed.

Himself the son of a factory worker, Abbé was a strong believer in industrial democracy. He paid high wages to all his staff, and also brought in a profit-sharing plan. He believed in guidance rather than control, and tended to set loose targets and ask his workers to meet them while giving them freedom in the execution of their tasks. Well in advance of other firms at the time, he also set up a sick pay fund and a company pension scheme, and introduced paid holidays. The social welfare model at Carl Zeiss was later used as a model by the German government when introducing its own social reforms.

The Carl Zeiss model survived until the end of the Second World War, when Jena became part of East Germany and the company passed into government control. The culture of innovation was dismantled. For a period of about forty years, however, Carl Zeiss Jena was one of the most innovative companies in the world, highly successful and the envy of its competitors. That success was built on a culture of collaboration created and guided by an ethical leader who believed in his company as a force for good.

Oneida Community

The Oneida Community was founded at Oneida, New York, in 1848 as a utopian socialist commune. The Community practised self-sufficiency, and all its members were required to work. A range of craft industries were developed, not all of them successful, but in the 1870s the Community also began making high-quality silver-plate tableware, a venture which proved immediately successful as the American middle class was expanding rapidly and there was a strong market. Initially all work was done by community members, but as the business grew the Community began employing workers; by 1870 Oneida was employing more than 200 people from outside the commune.

In 1879 the original Community dissolved and its leaders took the somewhat unusual step of converting the commune to a joint-stock company, giving shares to all adult members of the former community. Pierrepont Noyes, the managing director and son of the commune's founder, set about modernizing and growing the business. At the same time, he was determined not to sacrifice the venture's values in the pursuit of profit. Indeed, he believed that those original ideals of equality and democracy could be turned to the advantage of both the workers and the business as a whole.

Noyes saw employee welfare not in terms of philanthropy but as a duty. He once remarked that employers should 'make no welfare moves from fear, but always and only because you believe that company success should add to the comfort and happiness of every member of the working group', and that 'when your employees really believe that you take a practical interest in their welfare and that you mean what you say, you will have acquired an asset money alone could never buy'.[5] That did not mean Noyes was a soft touch. In 1899 he broke a strike at the company's Niagara Falls workshop, not because he was opposed to unions – quite the contrary – but because he did not believe the Oneida ethic could work in a unionized shop. Fiercely loyal to his own workers, he asked for and usually got their strong loyalty in turn.

And this in turn gave Oneida a competitive strength unknown to many of its rivals. During one economic downturn, Noyes called his workers together and asked them to take a voluntary pay cut, promising to restore wages as soon as the market turned up again. Trusting him, the workforce agreed unanimously, even giving Noyes a round of applause at the end of the meeting. Oneida survived that crisis and went on to became one of the leading tableware makers in the United States, sailing through the Wall Street Crash of 1929 which accounted for several of its rivals and continuing to expand through the

Great Depression. Oneida also became one of the most respected brands in the country, valued by customers for its quality. Today it remains one of the largest tableware producers in the United States.[6]

Infosys

Infosys, the Indian-based IT giant, has some unusual recruitment policies. Having hired someone, the company then takes great care to fit the job around the person, rather than attempting to hammer square pegs into round holes. The company believes that it has an ethical responsibility to ensure its employees are in jobs that suit them; and further, that having spent a great deal of money hiring and training people, it makes sense to get the best out of them.

If at the end of the first appraisal period a new employee is found to be underperforming, Infosys does not fire them (unless there has been genuine malfeasance). Rather, the company once again takes responsibility and accepts that it got things wrong. It hires good people; therefore, if an employee is underperforming, they must have been put into the wrong job. After interviews and analysis, a new job is found for the employee and they are moved to a new position.

If a second appraisal finds that there is still underperformance, the process repeats itself and the employee is moved again. Only if there is a third successive record of underperformance does Infosys accept that the wrong person may have been hired in the first place, and terminate the contract.

This is both an ethical and a practical position which aims to get the best out of people while also respecting their dignity. Partly as a result of this, Infosys has very loyal and committed employees who know they will not automatically be punished if they fail to hit targets. Treating people with respect has led to high commitment and high productivity.

7

Value and Trust: Customers

'The customer is always right.' 'The customer is king (or queen).' 'Client first.' We hear the words all the time, read them in annual reports and mission statements, hear them dripping from the lips of corporate PR agents, but how often do we really believe it?

Too often, the relationship between company and customer is – like the relationship between company and worker – exploitative and one-sided. 'Yield management' is the rather brutal term first pioneered in the airline industry which calculated how much revenue can be squeezed out of each passengers, just as farmers might calculate how many pounds of potatoes they can harvest from each acre of land.

Unsurprisingly, customers don't like being treated like potatoes. When Deutsche Bahn, the German railway company, began experimenting with yield management techniques in 2002, customers protested vigorously and some switched to other forms of transport. The company was forced to back down.

Economists like to talk about perfect markets, where all information is freely available and is reflected in the price. In reality, information asymmetries are omnipresent, and nearly always favour the seller. As customers, we go into most transactions nearly blind. All we have to go on is our own previous experience of the product and the brand, plus what we might have heard about it from others who have made the same purchase. We have to trust that the seller is not ripping us off.

For many people, marketing and advertising have become synonymous with false promises by companies. My own MBA students – who are, let us not forget, studying to become managers and business leaders – are highly sceptical about advertising, none more so than those who have a marketing background. The public are equally cynical. Naomi Klein's book *No Logo* became a best-seller because it tapped into that vein of cynicism; and, if we are absolutely honest, much of what she says is true.[1] Not everything, but quite a lot.

So, why put up with this? Why accept marketing and advertising techniques that many of us, business leaders included, know are ethically dubious and morally damaging? When will we stop treating customers like potatoes, and begin to treat them as what they really are: partners in value creation?

Markets and value

We talk about companies creating value, but this is not strictly speaking true. Companies create *potential* value for customers, but that value only becomes realized when the customer makes a purchase and uses or consumes the product. Only then does the product take on meaning for them. Only then does it affect their lives, and only then is true value created.

That simple premise lies at the heart of both economics and marketing. The company does not create value, and neither unaided does the customer. It is the act of exchange in the market, and its consequences, that creates value.

This means that whenever we talk about value creation, the customer must ipso facto be part of the equation. The decisions that we make about products and services affect customers because they are stakeholders in the business, and that brings in the moral and ethical dimension. We have a responsibility to customers that goes beyond the mere generation of transactions and yield management.

First and foremost, customers need to know they can trust the products and services they are buying. Among other things, they need to know that their purchase:

- Won't kill them
- Won't make them ill or cause harm to themselves or members of their family
- Will actually do what the label says it will do
- Will actually do what the customer wants it to do
- Is priced in line with the value that it will realistically create
- Will, through its use, result in satisfaction in some form for the customer and their family

When we advertise products and sell them, we have a moral responsibility to tell the truth. When telecoms companies advertise broadband packages capable of a certain speed, and then provide services that aren't capable of achieving half that speed, then those companies are committing a breach of trust. And when white goods manufacturers sell products supposedly guaranteed as safe, but which are actually capable of causing fires that devastate entire tower blocks – and, knowing this, continue to offer those products on the market – then they are stepping a long, long way over the ethical line.

Brands and trust

But there is more to ethical relationships with customers than just telling the truth.

Naomi Klein notes how logos have become fashion statements and many of us crave them for their own sake, but in fact the first logos were in effect a form of quality assurance kite mark. The first known brand marks come from

China in the tenth century, but by the eighteenth century it was common for reputable manufacturers to mark their goods in some way to distinguish them from cheap imitations and forgeries.[2]

Today, Charles Babbage is best known as one of the founding fathers of modern computing, but being a good nineteenth-century polymath he was keenly interested in many things, the economics of markets among them. In his book *The Economy of Machinery and Manufactures*, Babbage spells out what a brand does. Whenever we make purchases, he says, we are taking a risk. For all we know, when we buy a pound of tea, what we are really buying is half an inch of tea leaves covering a pound of sawdust. By the time we get our purchase home and discover the truth, it is too late. The brand mark assures us that we are buying from an honest producer who will not cheat us.[3]

Musing on the same theme a few decades later, William Lever described how he picked Sunlight as the name for his new soap product. He wanted a name that promised brightness and cleanness, but he also wanted the name to connote clarity and trust. Sunlight was intended to be a cheap, pure product, free of harmful adulterations and safe to use.[4] As we saw above, Henry Heinz put those same values at the core of his food brand.

Today, we labour under the delusion that legislation protects us from food impurities – the food poisoning epidemic in the United States in 2018 should give us pause for thought on that score[5] – but we run many other risks when we buy products that we don't know, or even ones that we think we do know. Missold pensions and payment protection insurance, faulty automobile parts, tumble dryers that start fires; the list goes on. We still rely on brands to send us signals about quality and trust, only sometimes the brand lets us down.

As consumers, we are anxious and eager to find brands we know we *can* trust; and if it turns out that our trust is justified, we tend to be loyal and stick with those brands because we know they will give us what we want. And, of course, this applies to more than just safety. Our reasons for buying brands are complex: self-esteem, and the need to belong to a group and share its identity, are also often part of the decision-making process. We need brands we can trust to deliver on these levels too.

More broadly, marketing and advertising can also be used to provide basic information about the product and what it does. In the view of Paul Cherington, one of the founding fathers of modern marketing theory, customer education should be marketing's primary function.[6] Encouraging customers to buy something they don't really understand might work for a short while, but sooner or later customers will start to see through the trick. Telling them what the product can do and what value it can create for them is a much better way of establishing the customer relationship.

At National Cash Register, John Patterson's salesmen would spend anything up to a week with potential customers, teaching them how to operate the cash machine and showing them its functions and utility. Only when the customer fully understood the product would the salesmen suggest a purchase. In my view, today's smartphone makers could take a leaf out Patterson's book. But then, I'm probably just getting old.

The point is that brands *can*, if they are perceived as being honest and uncynical, become a powerful source of trust and reassurance.

Consumers and the ethical value chain

We talk all the time about how important customers are, and yet most business leaders, especially senior ones, spend hardly any time with their customers. There are companies – Marks & Spencer being an example – that still require their directors to spend one day a quarter, or even one day a month, on the shop floor interacting with customers, but these companies are relatively rare.

Lacking any form of direct contact with customers, how then are leaders meant to establish their ethical position, or communicate their values and standards? Here we see why it is so vitally important to have committed staff who have shared and internalized those values. Staff are our ambassadors. It is they who see customers every day, talk to them, influence them and demonstrate what our values and beliefs are.

Also, just because the leaders don't see their customers doesn't mean the reverse is true. High-profile business leaders are often in the spotlight; especially, as we saw in Chapter 1, when things go wrong. Authenticity and walking the walk are again crucial. Leaders must do more than just talk about the company's morals and values; they must live them. Leaders are in effect living brands, symbolizing what the company stands for.

The process is not a quick one. It takes time for customers to get to know a brand and learn to trust it. They will base their opinion on personal experience, their own and that of friends and family members, or fellow members of social media networks. People don't just listen to the stories the company tells them; they also listen to the stories they tell each other. The company is just one actor on a sometimes crowded stage. Getting the message across requires time, patience and repetition. Tell the story of what you stand for, and keep telling it over and over again. Then, live those values.

Just like employees, customers also want to be authentic. They want their lives to have meaning. From a marketing perspective, that means connecting our customer offering – what we sell, how and where and when we sell it – with the hopes and aspirations of customers. Psychographic research can help us create profiles, but the real learning comes from personal, direct contact with customers. Procter & Gamble employs researchers who spend hours with customers, talking with them, accompanying them to the supermarket, observing their lives, looking into their eyes and listening to their stories. The purpose is not to learn what customers think about soap. The purpose is to understand them as people, so that the company has some idea of what value they are expecting and how to go about creating it.

And then, of course, we must monitor performance and make sure we are treating everyone ethically and fairly, and we must ensure continuity over time, so that the ethical standards by which we treat customers do not slip and the brand does not diminish. Here too, having committed staff is crucial. Look after your staff, and they will look after your customers for you.

So, I hear you ask, what is 'ethical' about this? Isn't this just good marketing? Yes, of course, it is. This is exactly what we as marketers should be doing, every day; this, and not yield management. Treating customers ethically and fairly is the best way to build relationships of trust which will create long-term value. And, if you are still sceptical, here are three cases of companies that did just that.

ESTABLISHING THE ETHICAL POSITION

Understanding what the customer wants, establishing trust, setting quality standards

COMMUNICATING VALUES AND STANDARDS

Using marketing and advertising honestly to convey the values and standards; authenticity

MOTIVATING OTHERS

Demonstrating value and quality, meeting customer needs

MONITORING ETHICAL PERFORMANCE

Monitoring quality of products and service, encouraging employees to do the same

ENSURING CONTINUITY

Upholding the ethical position, ensuring standards do not slip, encouraging employees to do the same

---

FIGURE 4 *The ethical value chain: customers.*

Tanishq

Tanishq is the jewellery division of Titan, the Indian watch manufacturer described in Chapter 4. It is India's largest jewellery retail chain, with more than 150 stores across India. The company has made a point of reaching down from the high-end market to middle-class market segments in smaller Indian cities.

Unlike in Europe, where gold and silver jewellery must comply with strict quality standards regarding purity, in India there are no guarantees of quality. Fakes abound, and unscrupulous sellers often pass off jewellery with little or no precious metal content. From its inception, Tanishq sought to develop a reputation for trustworthiness and honesty. It offers guarantees of purity, and, through its branding and promotional material, constantly reassures customers that what they are buying is genuine.

As part of this commitment, Tanishq introduced testing stations into many of its retail outlets, where customers can test their gold jewellery and check that it is genuine. This service is offered free of charge to anyone who walks in the door. You need to be a Tanishq customer; people can bring jewellery bought from a street trader or in the marketplace and test it for purity – and then, if the item proves to be a fake, take the test results back to the vendor to demand redress. Tanishq does not profit directly from this service, but it does continue to build its reputation as a reliable company that cares about its customers, and can be trusted by them. By striving to bring honesty into an industry noted for fakes and forgeries, Tanishq is creating a unique reputation and building strong bonds with its customers.

Thomas Cook

Thomas Cook, the company that pioneered the concept of mass tourism, actually had its origins in the temperance movement. Its founder, a carpenter and campaigner against alcohol named Thomas Cook, began organizing local excursions to attend temperance meetings in Leicester, but soon realized that pleasure excursions could be profitable as well. By the mid-1840s he was organizing travelling parties to destinations across the Midlands. The business really took off with the Great Exhibition of 1851, when Cook organized package tours including railway travel, hotels and meals for people wanting to travel to London to see the Exhibition. By 1855 he was running tours to Paris, and by the 1860s his company was sending tour groups across Western Europe.

The following decade saw the first tours to the Middle East and Egypt, then America and India. Cook even got involved in the Muslim pilgrimage trade, organizing tours to take pilgrims to Mecca. By 1890 the company employed 1,700 people worldwide and was selling more than 3 million package tours every year.

Cook succeeded because he understood his market. Middle-class and prosperous working-class families who would enjoy the chance to travel were deterred from doing so by two key risk factors: lack of familiarity with local customs, language and cultures, and uncertainty about the costs of travel. Cook introduced 'conducted tours', whereby an agent familiar with the local area would accompany the party at all times and solve any travel-related problems as they arose. The agents were responsible for the health and safety of customers; it was their job to ensure that they enjoyed their holiday, but also to keep them safe and see that they came to no harm.

Cook or his senior employees always travelled the route of each excursion in advance, inspected hotels and facilities and made prior arrangements, paid for all facilities to be used and even wrote guidebooks for the use of his customers, the ancestors of the modern travel guides such as Lonely Planet. By familiarizing themselves with the tour routes and inspecting facilities, Cook and his agents were providing a guarantee of quality.

Cook also developed the concept of the all-inclusive holiday package. Each member of a tour paid a flat fee which included all travel, accommodation and food. Cook thus assumed the entire cost risk of the excursion. This was important because it meant that travellers knew exactly how much they would have to pay, and there would be no unwelcome surprises.

In the travel business, the Thomas Cook name became synonymous with trust. Customers knew what they were getting and knew that they would have a quality experience; if problems did arrive when travelling, the company would deal with them. Hotels, railways and shipping companies likewise learned that Thomas Cook was a trustworthy partner that always kept its promises. The company always behaved responsibly and ethically towards both customers and partners, and, as a result, trust became the key value that underpinned the Thomas Cook brand.[7]

But trust, once gained, can be easily lost. In 2006, two children on a Thomas Cook holiday in Corfu died of carbon monoxide poisoning in their holiday accommodation. The inquiry into the case dragged on for nearly a decade, during which Thomas Cook was accused of failing to accept responsibility for the case, and of failing to apologize to the family of the bereaved. A full apology was finally issued, but only after the conclusion of the inquest in 2015. For some, this was too little, too late. Social network Mumsnet pulled Thomas Cook's advertising from its site, and a boycott of the company was threatened.[8]

'When companies go into defence mode, they stop being human', said one public relations expert. 'The fundamental fact is that they [Thomas Cook] were not human. They needed to show they understood some of the pain caused.'[9] Thomas Cook survived the crisis, but trust in the brand has been eroded. It will take a long time for that trust to be restored.

Nationwide

With origins going back to the nineteenth century, Nationwide is the largest building society in the UK. Despite many pressures, Nationwide has held steadfastly to its roots and traditional values, and has not been afraid to push back against the rest of the financial services sector in order to do so.

During the 1980s and 1990s many UK building societies demutualized and converted to banks. Nationwide's leaders refused to follow suit, fending off several attempts to demutualize, including a closely fought referendum of members on the subject. The society argued, successfully, that it would be better placed to serve customers' needs as a mutual society than as a bank. Conversion to bank status would hand too much control to big shareholders, and there was a real danger that the dominant ethos would become profit-making rather than service to the community.

Nationwide also defended its customers in other ways. During the 1990s Barclays Bank threatened to introduce charges for cash machine use by non-Barclays customers, including those of Nationwide. The building society fought back, threatening Barclays with legal action on behalf of its own customers and members. Eventually the threat was withdrawn.

Standing by its values has enhanced Nationwide's reputation with all its stakeholders. In 2017, Nationwide won the Which? award for Banking Brand of the Year, awarded for trustworthiness and customer service, and in 2016, the *Sunday Times* put Nationwide third in its list of top twenty-five best companies to work for.[10]

8

Virtue and Wealth: Community

According to polling agency Gallup, only about one in five Americans trusts big business.[1] Europeans are even more sceptical. Higher levels of trust have been recorded in some emerging economies, but even so, I have found no country where a majority of people trust big business.

More people trust small businesses, although there is no evidence that small businesses are any more ethical or moral than their larger counterparts. This higher level of trust reflects the fact that small businesses are more likely to be embedded in the community. People can see what they are doing, talk to their employees, judge their actions; and, importantly, make their feelings known quickly and clearly, with a fair assurance that they will be listened to. Small businesses know they need the trust of the communities in which they operate. Without that trust, no one will buy their products and no one will work for them. A small firm that forfeits the trust of its neighbours faces a future that is short and bleak.

With growth often comes a disconnect. The society that spawned the business and gave it life becomes remote. The attention of management focuses on a few key relationships: shareholders, customers, employees. The wider world becomes nothing more than a dim horizon, vaguely comprehended but not really understood. When the public reacts with anger, as they did during the Facebook data scandal, the company's first reaction is often one of astonishment. Mark Zuckerberg's hesitant response was not down to any feeling of guilt or complicity; his public remorse for what had happened was genuine. But Facebook executives had got used to be adored and admired for their success. People had made Hollywood films about them. To be cast as villains was an unexpected shock.

Facebook's executives had lost touch with their constituents, not just their service users but the wider community. They failed to realize the concern and worry that many feel in an era of big data, when privacy and personal security seem under threat as never before. They had lost touch with the community.

Corporate leaders need to find ways of recapturing that small business feeling. 'Think global, act local' has never been more apt as a maxim. Take the global overview by all means, but get back in touch with the communities you came from, where you work, where you operate, where you have a stake in the market. This is what Tata does very well in India, reaching out and touching communities, seeing people as individuals. Interestingly, Tata has struggled to replicate this recipe outside of India.[2]

Do no evil

The first step in building relationships with communities is reducing or eliminating negative externalities that affect those communities. Here again, actions speak far louder than words. If we hold out the hand of friendship, telling communities we want to work with them and invest in them, while simultaneously dumping toxic waste into the ground water, we are unlikely to make much progress.

Nor is it always just a matter of cleaning up our own mess. We saw earlier how, in the aftermath of the scandal of contaminated milk in China that killed some children and made hundreds of others sick, Tetra Pak stepped in and helped clean up the entire supply chain, offering consultancy, training and advice to other members of the chain. Often this support was provided for free. That investment in a clean supply chain not only propped up the entire dairy industry and helped it get through the scandal, but it also won Tetra Pak a dominant position in the packaging market – and the respect of the Chinese people, who saw Tetra Pak as a friend.

On the other side of the coin is Martin Winterkorn, former CEO of Volkswagen AG, who in the words of *Forbes* magazine, 'urged European regulators not to overburden the automotive industry with excessive emissions targets, citing a lack of time to develop fuel-efficient technology and the economic downturn as major concerns'.[3] This was at a time when worries about the health impacts of air pollution caused by diesel cars in particular were beginning to mount. The tone Winterkorn set percolated down through the company, and in 2015 it was revealed that Volkswagen engineers had developed a 'defeat device' that would disguise the levels of emissions from Volkswagen diesel cars during tests. The real level of emissions was far higher than the tests showed.

This was by no means the first time a car company had broken the rules concerning emissions. Volkswagen itself had been fined heavily for doing so in 1973.[4] The repercussions for Volkswagen, however, have been particularly severe. The day after news of the scandal broke, Volkswagen shares lost 20 per cent of their value on the Frankfurt stock exchange, and the price continued to drop over the next year. Sales were also badly hit, especially in the United States, and sales of diesel cars in particular have not recovered. Around $25 billion in fines have been levied, with the prospect of more to come. On 3 May 2018, Martin Winterkorn was charged with attempting to defraud the US government.[5]

Cleaning up our act, getting rid of negative externalities, is a good form of defence. If we have done nothing wrong, if we can invoke the sunlight test and defend our actions in public as moral and honourable, then it becomes much harder for people to attack us. But once again, there is much more to it than

ESTABLISHING THE ETHICAL POSITION

*Commitment to the community, and to providing value for the people/
reducing externalities*

COMMUNICATING VALUES AND STANDARDS

Telling the story of who you are and what kind of company we want to be

MOTIVATING OTHERS

*Finding ways to engage with people and support them, so they will also
support us*

MONITORING ETHICAL PERFORMANCE

*Watching the impact of what we do, what is valued and what is an
externality*

ENSURING CONTINUITY

Upholding the ethical position, ensuring standards do not slip

FIGURE 5 *The ethical value chain: community.*

that. Genuine investment in people and communities can become a source of competitive advantage right across the board.

Investing in people and places

'We don't do philanthropy', one executive at Tata Steel told me. At first glance this was rather surprising, given what the company does do: health care and education provided to 600 villages around Jamshedpur, a state-of-the-art sports facility open not just to workers and their families but the Jamshedpur community, a heritage centre that aims to preserve and celebrate the fast-vanishing cultures of the Adivasi people, India's original inhabitants; the list goes on and on. When I last visited Jamshedpur the company was in a state of great excitement; a young Adivasi woman from one of the villages nearby, who had gone to university on a Tata scholarship, had just been elected to the Lok Sabha, the lower house of India's parliament; the first woman of her ethnic group to be elected.

What the executive meant is that this kind of community support is not something Tata Steel does as an adjunct. It is built into its core business model, and costed as a business activity. Building community relationships is what Tata does. There are many advantages, including a loyal and committed workforce dedicated to quality and innovation, but that is not the primary reason why Tata supports communities. It does so because of virtue ethics. This is part of Tata's DNA, parts of its reason for existence. 'Profit', as another executive told me, 'is a byproduct of what we do'.[6]

'To really win back trust, companies must show their dedication to a broader purpose', says Eduardo Leite, chairman emeritus of international law firm Baker Mackenzie. 'They need to prove they are not just driven by quick profits, but also by values. This is the new order in the wake of the turbulent global times of the past five years.' Leite argues that this much more than just a matter of compliance with the law. Companies 'must also be seen to be doing the right thing.' He goes on to call for 'new laws, new ways of ensuring all parties can look each other in the eye and know they will get a fair reward for a fair transaction. In short, that they can trust each other'.[7]

I agree with Leite on the need to rebuild trust, but I am not convinced that we need more laws in order to do so. A deontological approach will only take us so far. Companies need to sit down and look at the consequences of their actions, good and bad, and see what impact these have on their business model and their long-term prosperity. The business case for building relationships with the community would seem to me to be self-evident. But beyond that, there is also virtue ethics, what kind of person or corporation we want to be. Do we know in our hearts what is the right thing to do? If the answer is yes, what is stopping us from doing it?

Demonstrating commitment

Building that trust and demonstrating that commitment take us back to the ethical value chain. We need first to look at the benefits and externalities that our operations provide to, or inflict upon, the communities where we work. Second, we need to take a position as to what we are going to do to both add value and reduce externalities. The value we decide we will provide establishes our ethical position.

Getting the message across is not always easy. Distrust and suspicion have been building up for a long time, and ramped up sharply after the 2008 financial crisis. The steady stream of new scandals, Uber and Facebook, Volkswagen and Oxfam and Weinstein, only reinforces the cynicism. In the present climate talk is cheap, and likely to be ineffective. Action is necessary. Set out a programme and then start carrying it out. Be authentic. Walk the walk.

Just as with employees – who, after all, very often live in and are members of the communities we are discussing – example sets the tone. Once people see that what we are doing has a positive impact on their lives, be it providing education to poor children, handing over land to create sports facilities or wildlife refuges, supporting libraries and community events, they will begin to understand we really do mean what we say. With understanding comes the beginning of trust. And just as with employees and customers too, the best way of motivating communities to trust us is to help them achieve what they want to do.

And, of course, relationship building is a continuous process. Care is needed to make sure the organization continues to fulfil its promises and do what it says it will do. Performance does need to be monitored. Again, though, if employees are sufficiently committed, then performance monitoring and ensuring continuity can become light-touch activities. Just as employees will, given the right encouragement and empowerment, build relationships with customers, so too they will build relationships with communities.

Supporting communities is partly a matter of what goes around comes around. If we support them, then they will support us with favourable public opinion and good word-of-mouth. If we take up an adversarial position, then we must not be surprised if communities fight back. But even more, there is once again the virtue ethics position. Do we really want to run companies that everyone hates? Do we want to work for them? Surely it is more satisfying to run a business that is respected and admired. Mark Zuckerberg clearly thinks so. What a pity he took his hand off the tiller, and let Facebook drift.

Shanghai Volkswagen

Shanghai Volkswagen was one of the earliest and most famous joint ventures between a Western and a Chinese company. Established in 1984 between the Shanghai Automotive International Company and Volkswagen, it was business that seemed ahead of its time. There were few paved roads in China, few petrol stations and few people with the disposable income to buy a car.

However, Volkswagen, the moving force behind the venture, saw a different future ahead. Volkswagen's leaders believed that China's economy would grow, and, with it, so would middle-class incomes. Volkswagen stated repeatedly that it was committed to helping China develop. It worked with the Chinese government and Chinese partner companies to develop not just a market for cars, but an entire industry and infrastructure. Volkswagen was eager to work with local partners, and by 1993, 85 per cent of the components in the cars it made in China were sourced locally. This helped create jobs, and prosperity.

At the beginning, Shanghai Volkswagen concentrated on the two markets that did already exist: government car fleets and taxis. Its move into the taxi market was particularly successful. The famous red Volkswagen Santana taxi became a ubiquitous sight on the streets of Shanghai and many other cities. By

2000, 53 per cent of all the cars on the road in China were made by Shanghai Volkswagen. The company turned around most of the profit it made and reinvested it in China. No profits at all were repatriated to Volkswagen until 1993, nine years after the venture was established, and even after that date the level of inward investment remained very high. The Chinese authorities, and the Chinese people, noted this commitment.

Competition did eventually come, in the form of other foreign ventures, including General Motors and Honda, and domestic car brands include Chery and Geely. By 2005 Shanghai Volkswagen's market share fell from 53 per cent to 15 per cent. But the Chinese public continued to regard Volkswagen with great affection, and brand awareness remained very high. New investment by Volkswagen saw new plants opening, and the elimination of all imported components; from 2008, all Shanghai Volkswagen cars were 100 per cent made in China. Sales surged once more.

Shanghai Volkswagen recognized from an early stage that what the Chinese valued most was commitment to their country. They were suspicious, and rightly so, of foreign brands that came to China just to make a fast buck. If they were to succeed, Western companies had to show that they were there not to make money, but to help the Chinese people achieve their aspirations and make their country great once again. Those that committed to that goal, like Shanghai Volkswagen, were rewarded with deep loyalty. Those that did not tended to wither on the vine.[8]

In closing, it is ironic that Volkswagen, which has demonstrated such strong commitment to the community in China, signally failed to do so in its European and American markets. The emissions scandal referred to above showed Volkswagen as just another selfish company prepared to put sales and profits ahead of the needs of the community. That has come back to bite them, of course. But it is interesting to see how two such different attitudes can prevail in the same company, without apparently anyone noticing the paradox.

Fairmont Yangcheng Lake

Yangcheng Lake is a popular holiday resort near Shanghai. By 2013 there were more than twenty luxury hotels in the district, of which Fairmont Yangcheng Lake was the only foreign-owned hotel. Fairmont also owns or manages three other hotels in China.

Founded in 1907, Fairmont Hotels & Resorts has a long track record of working with local communities to achieve sustainable growth, and had been doing so long before 'corporate social responsibility' became a fashionable term. Part of Fairmont's global philosophy is the education of both staff and guests about the environment, history and culture of the areas in which it operates. This philosophy has been transferred to China and adapted to local needs. There are now major projects across all the company's properties aimed at conserving energy and reducing energy usage, reducing consumption of gas and water, reducing packaging, recycling kitchen waste and, where possible, using organic or sustainably sourced food in its restaurants. 'Green committees' in every hotel give employees a chance to develop and implement their own ideas, and also serve as a channel for staff education on sustainability.

Local sourcing is a key part of Fairmont's philosophy. Fairmont recognizes the importance of its business to local communities, especially in terms of local purchasing, and strives wherever possible to purchase local products and to help the economies of these communities. Fairmont also collaborates with suppliers to help reduce their CO_2 emissions. Fairmont's Yangcheng Lake Hotel has gone so far as to develop its own vegetable supplier, Yangcheng Lake Farm, which is owned by the Kunshan city government and managed by Fairmont. The Farm grows everything from seasonal vegetables popular in Shanghai to Western herbs. More generally, Fairmont buys 80 per cent of its food locally, within a radius of approximately twenty miles from each hotel.

This policy provides tangible benefits for local farmers and supports the local economy, but it has been beneficial in other ways too. Food, especially fresh, nourishing food, plays a very important role in Chinese culture. The quality of fresh vegetables at Fairmont has become a major draw, and the gardens themselves have become a tourist attraction. Guests now come out from Shanghai on special food holidays to sample dishes created by a specialist vegetarian chef. The hotel has also begun selling vegetables not wanted for the kitchens, running a vegetable box distribution scheme in Shanghai.

More recently Fairmont has begun another project aimed at restoring the old waterways and canals around Yangcheng Lake. In former times these waterways were a source of fresh fish, and communities of fishermen made their livelihood from fishing there. A combination of water pollution from nearby industries and general neglect means the waterways have either become fouled or disappeared altogether. Working with local villages, Fairmont is reviving these waterways and restocking them with fish. It is hoped that the waterways will supply the hotel with its entire requirements for fresh fish, and this too will assist the development of the local community.

Fairmont sees no difference between investing in communities and supplying first-class hotel services to paying guests. Both are part of its core business model. At Yangcheng Lake, Fairmont's commitment to the community is well known and admired. That commitment is one reason why the Fairmont hotel has prospered and its business has grown in the face of tough competition from numerous local hotel chains. Service to community equates to competitive advantage.[9]

Saltaire

Titus Salt was a nineteenth-century cloth manufacturer, based in Bradford. He made his fortune through the weaving and sale of alpaca cloth, a complex and difficult process that yielded a very fine and durable cloth that at once became popular. By 1850 Salt owned six cloth factories in Bradford and was a very wealthy man.

Heavily polluted, Bradford was sometimes described as 'dirtiest city in Britain'. The city's factories were powered by steam, the boilers heated by coal, and smoke and soot poured constantly from hundreds of chimneys in and around the city. The river which flowed through the city was both the source of drinking water and the drain for its untreated sewage. Rates of infant mortality, even by the standards of the time, were very high and other diseases flourished. Average life expectancy was the lowest in the country.

In the early 1840s Salt launched a campaign for cleaner air in the city, but he failed to persuade his fellow mill owners to back him. Undeterred, he stood for mayor of Bradford and was elected to the post in 1848. He at once launched an inquiry into the state of the city's working-class housing, and was shocked at the conditions he found. In 1849 Bradford suffered a severe epidemic of cholera caused by the polluted waters, and much of Salt's efforts as mayor were devoted to dealing with this crisis.

In 1850, despairing of improving conditions in Bradford itself, Salt resolved to move his own operations out of the city. He did this partly in order to protect his own workers, and partly in hopes of persuading others to follow his example. His choice was a greenfield site three miles north of the city, where he intended to concentrate all his business operations on a single site. As well as state-of-the-art production facilities, the factory was designed to provide a safe and clean working environment. Ventilation was introduced to keep dust levels down, and the shafts and chains that drove the machinery were placed under the floors of the workshops in order to reduce noise.

Salt also built housing for his workers. The town of Saltaire eventually included housing for 4,500 workers and their families, schools, a hospital, a Congregational church and a Methodist chapel, shops, a community centre and alehouses for recreation. Clean water was provided from a purpose-built reservoir, and there were also a number of public bath houses. Saltaire provided a standard of accommodation far higher than that available to ordinary millworkers in the UK, and the settlement was studied by both industrialists and sociologists from at home and abroad. The success of Saltaire influenced both George Cadbury and William Lever in their later developments at Bourneville and Port Sunlight.

The combination of high-quality housing and state-of-the-art manufacturing technology was very successful. Salt enjoyed generally good relations with his workers, and, despite two brief strikes in the 1860s, which were settled peacefully, labour relations at Saltaire were far better than in most of the industry.

More broadly, Salt served as President of the Bradford Chamber of Commerce and continued to campaign for better public health and public education. His efforts finally paid off, and the Bradford city authorities took measures to provide better sanitation and clean drinking water. He was also an advocate of greater personal freedom and campaigned to extend the right to vote beyond its present narrow limits (men under the age of 30 – and, of course, all women of whatever age – were still denied the right to vote in England). He was also, quietly, a philanthropist and benefactor who gave away most of his personal fortune – according to some estimates, £500,000 – before his death. When he died in 1876, 100,000 people (virtually the entire population of Bradford) turned out to watch the funeral procession.[10]

Salt invested in his people and their community because he believed it was the right thing to do. He did reap rewards in the form of healthy productive workers, good labour relations and a reputation for being a trustworthy and caring man, but that was not his principal purpose. He urged reform and dipped into his own pocket to provide his workers with clean, safe homes and workplace because that was the kind of man he wanted to be.

9

Value Is What You Get: Shareholders

It is often forgotten, including by shareholders themselves, that shareholders do not own the companies in which they invest. They own the share capital of those companies, but they have no ownership of the assets. Owning shares in a brewery does not entitle you to free beer.

Too many shareholders still treat this as a distinction without a difference. The philosophy of shareholder value maximization, rooted in the Chicago School of economics, has dominated the discussion for many decades now. According to this view, as Chicago economist Milton Friedman put it, a company's sole duty is to return value to shareholders.[1] This means the shareholders are considered the most important – sometimes the only important – stakeholders in the business.

There are, however, several problems with this theory. First, prioritizing the interests of shareholders over those of employees, customers and the wider community is a recipe for conflict. When companies focus only on maximizing shareholder wealth, experience shows that this usually results in lower wages and worse working conditions, a reduction in customer quality and negative externalities for the community. The consequences are labour unrest, dissatisfied customers who vote with their feet and backlash from governments and regulators. The things that were supposed to save money so more wealth could be generated for shareholders end up costing more and adding still further to the pressures on management.

Second, the model inherently carries more risk. As William Lazonick and Mary O'Sullivan pointed out in an article a few years ago, the drive for shareholder value maximization pushes companies towards higher gearing, taking on more and more debt until in some cases they become unsustainable.[2]

Carillion, the construction and infrastructure firm that collapsed in January 2018 with debts of £900 million, is a case in point. Carillion symbolizes just about everything that is bad about the shareholder value maximization model: expansion at the expense of common sense, a reckless disregard for risk and an almost desperate drive for growth to placate shareholders. A parliamentary inquiry commented:

> Carillion's rise and spectacular fall was a story of recklessness, hubris and greed. Its business model was a relentless dash for cash, driven by acquisitions, rising debt, expansion into new markets and exploitation of suppliers ... The mystery is not that it collapsed, but that it lasted so long.[3]

For once, it is difficult to disagree with politicians.

In cases like Carillion, shareholders have a responsibility to move in sooner. When management has chosen a risky and dangerous strategy, shareholders need to call them out. Carillion's rapid growth doubtless did create shareholder value in the short term, but in the long term there is only a gaping empty hole where value should have been. Failures like Carillion represent waste, a lost opportunity to build something that would create far more value over the long term.

Price is what you pay, said Warren Buffett; value is what you get. Investment strategies need to focus more on real long-term value. And investors need to realize that they too are part of a community. The value they receive, the return on capital invested, is created by employees and customers, not by management. Shareholders, just like business leaders, need to look after their stakeholders and ensure they are happy. Otherwise, the goose that lays the golden eggs will soon stop laying.

Long-termism

One of the most outspoken foes of short-termism over the past few years has been Dominic Barton, managing director of McKinsey & Company. The head of the world's biggest management consulting firm spends a great deal of his time trying to persuade big investors to see the world through a different lens. His article in *Harvard Business Review* in 2011, 'Capitalism for the Long Term', was a clarion call:

> Executives must infuse their organizations with the perspective that serving the interests of all major stakeholders – employees, suppliers, customers, creditors, communities, the environment – is not at odds with the goal of maximizing corporate value; on the contrary, it's essential to achieving that goal.[4]

In a later article, Barton and Mark Wiseman called for a fundamental shift in the investment climate based on four principles:

1 Invest after defining long-term objectives and focus on value creation

2 Unlock value through engagement and active ownership

3 Demand long-term metrics to inform decisions

4 Structure institutional governance to support a long-term approach[5]

In short, Barton is calling for shareholders to pull their seats up to the table and take responsibility for the governance of the firms in which they invest. Those firms, of course, would argue that it is shareholders who are putting the pressure on them to act in the short-term. That was true once, but as I remarked earlier, the days of shareholder value maximization are waning. It is still the dominant way of thinking in the United States – as editor of *Corporate Finance Review* from 1999 to 2016, I was very much involved in campaigning against value maximization and I saw how pervasive this way of thinking still is – and it still has a strong foothold in Britain.

Elsewhere in Europe, though, the tide is turning. Shareholders are beginning to ask for long-term value, and to insist that the views of other stakeholders are taken into account. The success of ethical investment funds and banks like Triodos has been noted, and more investors are shifting their position. And as Dominic Barton pointed out in 'Capitalism for the Long Term', Asia is already there. Asian companies and investors typically take a fifteen- to twenty-year time horizon. The focus on long-term value creation is one of the reasons why Asian economies have been so successful; and the failure to do so is one of the reasons why we are beginning to struggle.

In general, the Carl Icahns of this world are a dwindling breed, and it is possible that they will soon go the way of the triceratops and the velociraptor. To the next generation they will be nothing more than fossils, decorating museum walls.

The shareholder value chain

And as the shift in priorities and values continues, the time is right for companies to start engaging with shareholders, bringing them to the table and linking their needs for value with those of consumers, employees and the community. They will still face resistance, as the example of Paul Polman and Unilever demonstrates, but that resistance is declining.

Rather than taking an adversarial position towards shareholders – or, even worse, a position of supine acquiescence to their every demand – business leaders need to start collaborating with the owners of capital and encouraging them to participate in broader value creation. Investors are people too, and,

---

MOTIVATING OTHERS
Working together to seek opportunities for value creation for all parties

ESTABLISHING THE ETHICAL POSITION
Collaborative discussion to establish the ethical position; what kind or organization do we want this to be?

COMMUNICATING VALUES AND STANDARDS
Deeds are better than words. Create value. Walk the walk.

MONITORING ETHICAL PERFORMANCE
Resist pressures to go short term, and stay focused on the standards

ENSURING CONTINUITY
Upholding the ethical position, ensuring standards do not slip

---

FIGURE 6 *The ethical value chain: shareholders.*

just like employees, once they internalize the process of change they will become its whole-hearted supporters.

In this case, I think we need to adjust ethical value chain. The starting point here should be motivation. What have we to gain by working together? What additional value can we create, over and above what we already have?

Once shareholders have the basic idea on board, establishing the ethical position can become a collaborative process. There is no harm in challenging shareholders about their own ethical views. How do they see themselves? What kind of organization do *they* want to be? What kind of organization do they want to invest in? Encourage them to internalize the company's values and, at the same time, help spread and share those values.

When it comes to communicating, there is really only one option. Nobody trusts financial PR anymore, not even those who work for financial PR firms. Get out there and do what you have said you will do. Live the values, and create the value. Shareholders will judge you by your results, not by your promises.

10

Making Ethical Decisions

I once tried to estimate how many management frameworks there are in existence, but I quite quickly gave up on the idea. The answer is thousands, quite likely tens of thousands. There are frameworks for managing accounting processes, procurement, R&D, human resource management, health and safety, customer relationship management, conducting meetings, estimating the correct height of a computer monitor above a desk. I once worked with a man whose subordinates claimed he used a spreadsheet to tell him when to go to the toilet.

Inevitably, there are frameworks for making ethical decisions. The quality of these, as with all frameworks, varies considerably. Some are vague and valueless; others are quite useful – within limits.

We have a tendency to use frameworks as tick-box exercises. Work through all the elements in order, tick all the boxes and you should come out with the right answer. This is wrong, dangerously so. Real-life leadership and management are full of ambiguity and paradox, and grey areas abound. No framework can ever account for every possibility we may face. And nowhere is this more true than in ethics.

Frameworks *are* useful to help guide our thinking. They can act as checklists to remind us of the vital elements we must not forget. But simply checking every item off the list is not enough. We need always to look inside ourselves, to return to our moral compass and our own notions of right and good and virtue. The framework cannot make the decision for us. Only we can do that.

To give some idea of how frameworks can be useful, I shall discuss three commonly used frameworks which are, in my view, among the best out there. (You may disagree, and you are perfectly free to go and research frameworks on your own; I do not claim any superiority of judgement.) I then add a simplified framework which I believe is useful in everyday management and decision making. Feel free to test all these frameworks on some ethical problems or dilemmas you may have encountered. Alternatively, Appendix 1 offers six real-life dilemmas which you can use for practice and evaluation.

The Nash framework

THE NASH FRAMEWORK

1 Have you defined the problem accurately?
2 How would you define the problem if you stood on the other side of the fence?
3 How did this situation occur in the first place?
4 To whom and what do you give your loyalties as a person and as a member of the organization?
5 What is your intention in making this decision?
6 How does this intention compare with the likely results?
7 Whom could your decision or action injure?
8 Can you engage the affected parties in a discussion of the problem before you make your decision?
9 Are you confident that your position will be as valid over a long period of time as it seems now?
10 Could you disclose without qualms your decision or action to your boss, your CEO, the board of directors, your family, or society as a whole?
11 What is the symbolic potential of your action if understood? If misunderstood?
12 Under what conditions would you allow exceptions to your stand?[1]

'Whether you regard it as an unchecked epidemic or as the first blast of Gabriel's horn, the trend toward focusing on the social impact of the corporation is an inescapable reality that must be factored into today's managerial decision making', says Laura Nash. 'But for the executive who asks, "How do we as a corporation examine our ethical concerns?" the theoretical insights currently available may be more frustrating than helpful.'[2] Critical of the gap between abstruse ethical theory and the needs of businesses, her article 'Ethics Without the Sermon' offers a framework for making ethical decisions. Her twelve questions can be seen in the display box above. Let us now take a closer look at this framework and examine the questions.

1   *Have you defined the problem accurately?* 'How one assembles the facts weights an issue before the moral examination ever begins, and a definition is rarely accurate if it articulates one's loyalties rather than the facts', says Nash.[3] It is vitally important to know as many facts about the case as possible, and to be sure that we are judging them fairly and impartially. If, for example, we are assessing the conduct of an employee at work but are unaware of stresses he or she may be suffering outside of work, then we may be seeing only part of the problem, and thereby miss out on options for a possible resolution. It is important to take a holistic view.

2   *How would you define the problem if you stood on the other side of the fence?* As part of that holistic view, we must be sure we are seeing the problem from the perspective of any other stakeholder who is affected. Suppose we are proposing to build a new factory next to a rural village. How would we feel if we lived in that village? Taking all these perspectives into account is necessary, especially from a consequentialist perspective, if we are to assess value creation and externalities accurately.

3   *How did this situation occur in the first place?* What is the background? What decisions were taken prior to this point? How did we get here? Other analytical tools like the 'Five Whys' or 'What, So What, Now What?' can sometimes be useful. This too is part of the interrogation of the problem, to be sure that we have a full understanding and background.

4   *To whom and what do you give your loyalties as a person and as a member of the organization?* This question should help you discover whether you have any internal conflicts. 'The good news about conflicts of loyalty is that their identification is a workable way of smoking out the ethics of a situation and of discovering the absolute values inherent in it', says Nash. 'As one executive in a discussion of a Harvard case study put it, "My corporate brain says this action is O.K., but my non-corporate brain keeps flashing these warning lights." '[4]

5   *What is your intention in making this decision?* What value are you trying to create, and for whom? Make a list of the potential benefits of your decision, and who, consequentially, will share them out.

6   *How does this intention compare with the likely results?* Given past experience and what you know of the environment, do you think you will succeed in reaching your goals? What might prevent you from doing so? If you cannot do so, what will be the consequences?

7   *Whom could your decision or action injure?* This is not just a matter of what will happen if things go wrong, though, of course, a risk assessment should certainly be part of ethical decision making. But we also need to assess the negative externalities.

An aquaculture company's decision to open a shrimp farm on the coast of Thailand contributes to the local economy by providing jobs and boosting tax revenues. At the same time, cutting down mangrove

forests to make way for the farm exposes coastal villages to a greater
risk of flooding during storms. Any externalities like this must be
costed into the decision; otherwise, the decision will impact negatively
on other people, and that from a consequentialist perspective would be
bad.

Nash argues that we need to think about these issues before we
embark on new ventures, rather than waiting until something bad
happens and then trying to fix it. 'To exclude *at the outset* any policy
or decision that might have such results is to reshape the way modern
business examines its own morality. So often business formulates
questions of injury only after the fact in the form of liability suits.'[5]

8   *Can you engage the affected parties in a discussion of the problem before
    you make your decision?* If at all possible, this should be done. Making
    decision about what other people consider to be right and wrong, or
    good and bad, without consulting them itself has ethical implications.
    Yet too often we don't consult, says Nash, because we think that doing
    so would take too long or be too expensive. Not consulting and getting
    it wrong can be more expensive still.

9   *Are you confident that your position will be as valid over a long period
    of time as it seems now?* Will you look back in a month's time, or a
    year, or ten years, and still think you did the right thing? This is, of
    course, tricky because we cannot see into the future. But it is useful
    to ask oneself some what-if questions. Suppose the economy turns
    upwards and demand increases; will we still have done the right thing
    by downsizing and laying off employees? Suppose the law changes and
    the actions we deem ethical now are declared illegal; will we still feel
    our actions are justified? No firm answers to these questions will be
    possible, but asking them anyway helps us tease out some of the issues
    we may otherwise have overlooked.

10 *Could you disclose without qualms your decision or action to your boss, your CEO, the board of directors, your family, or society as a whole?* This is sometimes known as the 'sunlight test'. Should your actions become public knowledge, would you be happy to stand up and justify them? If you are summoned to testify before a House of Commons select committee, can you put your hand on your heart and say that if you had to do it over again, you would make the same decision?

11 *What is the symbolic potential of your action if understood? If misunderstood?* Regardless of what you intend, people will put their own spin your decisions and actions. 'A business decision', says Nash, 'has a symbolic value in signalling what is acceptable behavior within the corporate culture and in making a tacit contract with employees and the community about the rules of the game. How the symbol is actually perceived (or misperceived) is as important as how you intend it to be perceived.'[6]

12 *Under what conditions would you allow exceptions to your stand?* Consistency of behaviour is very important in terms of perceptions. As we saw in the Oxfam case at the beginning of the book, a legacy of decades of good work with poor and needy people counted for little when the public learned about sexual misconduct in Haiti. Standards, once set, must be upheld. At the same time, we must avoid the absurd extremes of the Legalist position and allow for at least some element of relativism. The soldier who leaves his post to save his leader should not be punished for acting without orders.

The Nash framework was designed to give business leaders a quick and relatively easy way of assessing situations and making decisions that are ethically sound. Nash deliberately eschews any relationship between her framework and traditional ethics theory, on the grounds that the latter is too abstruse and not relevant. Nevertheless, we can see elements of ethical theory here. The majority of the questions are skewed towards consequentialism – good outcomes – with some, such as questions 4 and 10 nodding towards virtue ethics.

Using this framework will not give us a simple yes/no answer at the end of the process. As Nash herself says, the twelve questions are designed to tease out the issues and make sure the implications are fully discussed. Personal experience of using and teaching this model suggests that it is quite a good starter for discussion, but with more complex dilemmas the discussion can actually end up muddying the waters and leaving people more confused than ever about what they should actually do.

The Josephson Institute framework

The Nash framework gives good results for relatively simple ethical dilemmas where the primary focus is on achieving a good outcome. A more complex framework comes from the Josephson Institute of Ethics. It consists of five steps with a number of sub-steps in each. Students sometimes complain that this framework is too cumbersome to use easily, but it is useful for digging deeper into the heart of ethical dilemmas, and has stronger roots in deontology and pragmatism than the Nash framework.

This framework comes from a booklet entitled *Five Steps of Principled Reasoning*, published by the Josephson Institute in 1999. The Institute has also published a later pamphlet, 'The Seven-Step Path to Better Decisions', which is greatly simplified even though it has more steps, but I think the original, presented in the box below, is stronger and more useful.

THE JOSEPHSON INSTITUTE FRAMEWORK

Clarify

1 Determine precisely what must be decided.
2 Formulate and devise the full range of alternatives.
3 Eliminate patently impractical, illegal and improper alternatives.
4 Force yourself to develop at least three ethically justifiable options.
5 Examine each option to determine which ethical principles and values are involved.

Evaluate

1 If any of the options requires the sacrifice of any ethical principle, evaluate the facts and assumptions carefully.
2 Distinguish solid facts from beliefs, desires, theories, suppositions, unsupported conclusions, opinions and rationalizations.
3 Consider the credibility of sources, especially when they are self-interested, ideological or biased.
4 With regard to each alternative, carefully consider the benefits, burdens and risks to each stakeholder.

Decide

1 Make a judgement about what consequences are most likely to occur.
2 Evaluate the viable alternatives according to personal conscience.
3 Prioritize the values so that you can choose which values to advance and which to subordinate.
4 Determine who will be helped the most and harmed the least.
5 Consider the worst-case scenario.
6 Consider whether ethically questionable conduct can be avoided by changing goals or methods, or by getting consent.
7 Apply the three 'ethics tests'
   7a Are you treating others as you would want to be treated?
   7b Would you be comfortable if your reasoning and decision were to be publicised?
   7c Would you be comfortable if your children were observing you?

Implement

1 Develop a plan of how to implement the decision.
2 Maximize the benefits and minimize the costs and risks.

> *Monitor and modify*
> 1 Monitor the effects of decisions.
> 2 Be prepared and willing to revise a plan, or take a different course of action.
> 3 Adjust to new information.[7]

Again, let us take each step in turn and examine it.

Clarify

1 Determine precisely what must be decided.

2 Formulate and devise the full range of alternatives.

3. Eliminate patently impractical, illegal and improper alternatives.

4 Force yourself to develop at least three ethically justifiable options.

5 Examine each option to determine which ethical principles and values are involved.

Similar to the Nash framework, Josephson argues that we need to be clear as to what decision we are being asked to make (and, I would add, why we are being asked to make it). In line with pragmatic thinking, Josephson also says that we should first consider all the options and, importantly, put at least three different options on the table for detailed discussion.

That is important, because sometimes it is only when we start considering multiple options that we begin to see clearly what we need to do. In their recent book *The Leading Brain*, Friederike Fabritius and Hans Hagemann examine one of the classic ways of making decisions, namely, tossing a coin.[8] Most of us have done this at one time or another, and most of us have experienced the same phenomenon. We are faced with a choice of turning left or right, so we toss the coin, heads for left, tails for right. The coin lands tails, telling us we should turn right. But the more we consider turning right, the more we realize that we are uneasy; the road is bad, or there could be danger. Instinct tells us to turn left. So we ignore the coin toss, which was meant to make the decision for us, and turn left anyway.

As Fabritius and Hagemann demonstrate, instinct in these cases is actually part of the brain's function. As soon as we become aware of a problem, the unconscious part of our mind goes to work on it and comes up with a decision. Meanwhile, we are deliberately using the conscious part of our mind to work on the same problem, hopefully using logic and reason, with a view to also reaching a decision. If both conscious and unconscious parts of our mind reach the same decision, we experience a feeling of pleasure or happiness; we feel good because we have made the right decision.

However, if the unconscious mind disagrees with the conscious mind, then a part of our brain called the insula, which controls bodily awareness, registers a threat and sounds a warning. The insula in turn is referring to another area of the brain, the basal ganglia, which is a storehouse for previous experience. 'Instinct', then, or 'gut feeling' is actually the brain's way of retrieving things from unconscious memory and bringing them to the fore.

When it comes to ethical decision making, we need to make sure that both our conscious and unconscious minds are brought to bear on the problem. Logic and analysis are highly important, but so are past experience, emotions and analysis. The right decision must *feel* right. Recall again the quote from Nash, above: 'My corporate brain says this action is O.K., but my non-corporate brain keeps flashing these warning lights.'

The non-corporate brain needs to be listened to, because it knows things the corporate brain does not. Looking at multiple alternatives is a more sophisticated way of tossing a coin. By evaluating these alternatives, we come to a clearer understanding.

As for ethical principles and values, these are the things we discussed in Chapter 2: right and wrong, fairness and equity, the creation of positive value and/or negative externalities for each stakeholder group. If there is time, make a list of the key principles involved, under positive and negative headings. Again, this list will not give you all the answers, but it will unlock thinking and force you to confront the ethical principles head on.

Evaluate

1 If any of the options requires the sacrifice of any ethical principle, evaluate the facts and assumptions carefully.

2 Distinguish solid facts from beliefs, desires, theories, suppositions, unsupported conclusions, opinions and rationalizations.

3 Consider the credibility of sources, especially when they are self-interested, ideological or biased.

4 With regard to each alternative, carefully consider the benefits, burdens and risks to each stakeholder.

This is the most important part of the Josephson framework, because it lays the foundations for the decision itself. Steps 2 and 3 concern the validity of the evidence we are using to make the decision. It is vital to establish the credibility of any source and understand any biases in thinking, including the biases of ourselves and our teams. Why do we think the way we do? What led to the conclusions we have reached? What is the possibility that our understanding of the situation is wrong? In the words of the medieval philosopher Peter Abelard, 'by doubting we come to examine, and by examining we reach the truth.'

Paradoxically, although we need to listen to the unconscious mind, we also need to be sure that we are dealing with facts and not rumours or vague suppositions. In the words of W. Edwards Deming, quality guru and philosopher in his own right, 'In God we trust; all others must bring data.'

Of course, telling fact from fiction is not always easy, and in some instances – like the shipyard case in Chapter 2 – other parties will conceal the facts or obstruct our view of them in a deliberate attempt to influence our decision. Facts can also be misinterpreted or misunderstood. Here is where the unconscious mind comes into its own, helping us to see through the fog. Facts are important, but they are not always enough. Self-belief and virtue must play a role too; and always, always we must consider that we might be wrong.

Step 4 is pure consequentialism, working out what the benefits and externalities will be for every stakeholder who is affected, or will be affected, by each option. Step 1, on the other hand, has its roots in deontology. What are the principles involved? What, if any, damage might be done to them by our actions? Is that damage acceptable? Are we ourselves willing to pay the price, if necessary, for doing what we believe to be right?

Decide

1   Make a judgement about what consequences are most likely to occur.

2   Evaluate the viable alternatives according to personal conscience.

3   Prioritize the values so that you can choose which values to advance and which to subordinate.

4   Determine who will be helped the most and harmed the least.

5   Consider the worst-case scenario.

6   Consider whether ethically questionable conduct can be avoided by changing goals or methods, or by getting consent.

7   Apply the three 'ethics tests'

   7a   Are you treating others as you would want to be treated?

   7b   Would you be comfortable if your reasoning and decision were to be publicised?

   7c.   Would you be comfortable if your children were observing you?

The actual decision-making process draws on all four of the theories of ethics we discussed in Chapter 2. In the evaluation phase, we looked at the range of possible consequences, positive value and negative externalities. Coming to a decision requires us to decide which are most likely and what the probable outcomes of each option will be. Step 4 also urges to consider *who* will benefit and *who* will be harmed. If there are externalities, are those who will be harmed be strong enough to bear the cost? If there is value, will it be distributed in a fair and equitable manner?

Personal conscience and values, our own virtue, also play a role here. Looking at the alternatives, which feels right? Which is most in line with our own personal values? What is our moral compass telling us? And, of course, there is the sunlight test. Equity and fairness dictate that we treat others as we would want to be treated ourselves, but as well as reciprocity there is a deeper need to be able to live with the consequence of our actions. Step 7c, 'would you be comfortable if your children were observing you?' is a particularly potent question to ask.

If the answer to this is 'no', then we really do need to stop and think again. For most of us, taking an action which we know to be unethical is corrosive, morally, psychologically, even physically. Once we cross the moral threshold once, it becomes much more likely that we will do so again, but that does not mean the process is easier or consequence-free. Studies have linked unethical behaviour to loss of self-esteem, depression, physical illnesses associated with depression and even self-harm and suicide.[9]

Pragmatically, we should also consider whether it is possible to alter the moral ecology to give ourselves more scope for action. The Josephson framework asks us to look at the worst-case scenario, but I would argue that we should go further and adopt the technique used in scenarios thinking, that is, for each option to consider the best case, the worst case, and then the most likely case, which will most of the time be somewhere between the two. While we always need to be mindful of the worst case, and have a plan in mind for how we will recover from failure if it happens, pragmatically we should devote most of our effort to considering the most likely case.

Ultimately, a decision must be made. The Josephson framework, like the Nash, will not tell us what decision to make. The moral choice is ours, and we must bear full responsibility for it. What the Josephson framework aims to do is (a) ensure we have as much reliable information, from trustworthy sources, as possible; (b) have looked at the issue from all angles and generated multiple option in order to ensure that we have worked through the issues fully, and are not just making the decision that is easiest, or cheapest, or benefits us and our friends; and finally (c) ensure that we have fully considered the consequences of all options to our stakeholders before we make the final choice.

Sometimes, that choice will appear to be easy, at least at first. The firm may have a cherished investment project, building a new factory or distribution centre, launching a new product line, on which management have set their hearts. But if, upon consideration, the ethical implications are too strongly negative and the externalities are too great, then the leaders need to put their hands up and cry stop.

Nor, having made a decision, should we regard ourselves as irrevocably committed to it. To repeat, we must always recognize the fact that we may be wrong. The situation may change, so that the original decision, although right at the time, is now no longer valid. We may have overlooked certain factors, or been given false information, meaning that our original assumptions were incorrect. New externalities may emerge that we had not foreseen. If so, we must have the courage and humility to admit failure, reconsider and, if necessary, pull back and choose another option.

THE GUNS OF AUGUST

Throughout the month of July 1914, there were intense diplomatic negotiations between the Great Powers of Europe: Britain, France and Russia, Austria-Hungary and Germany. Despite the best efforts of the diplomats, the negotiations failed, in large part because the national leaders believed war was inevitable. Once the orders to mobilize the armies and fleets had been given, they said, it was impossible to stop the process. There was nothing left to do but carry on and go to war. Everyone knew the consequences would be disastrous, but the few politicians who did have the courage to stand up and cry stop were shouted down by the others who insisted that war was inevitable. As a result, at the beginning of August, the First World War began and 17 million people died.[10]

Very few things in life are truly inevitable. There is always time to stop. All that is required is courage, and the ability to make other people listen.

Implement

1   Develop a plan of how to implement the decision.

2   Maximize the benefits and minimize the costs and risks.

Monitor and modify

1   Monitor the effects of decisions.

2   Be prepared and willing to revise a plan, or take a different course of action.

3   Adjust to new information.

I have put these two steps together because implementation and monitoring ought to go hand in hand. They should be inseparable.

Implementation happens just as it would with any project. An action plan is developed and carried out. As well as financial benefits and risks, we need to keep a constant eye on the value that is being created, and ensure that what we want to happen actually happens. This means watching out for unintended consequences and unexpected externalities. For example, if in the process of building a new plant the work teams create excessive noise pollution which harms the health of nearby communities, as leaders we need to step in and rectify the situation.

There is more to monitoring, however, than simply keeping the ship on course. By embracing an *action learning* approach, we can learn from experience and improve our decision-making capabilities. Action learning theory proposes that we learn far more from doing things ourselves than we do from studying or emulating the actions of others. In order to learn from experience, we need to reflect on what we have done and take a questioning approach, asking why we did what we did and whether we could have done things differently.[11]

The psychologist Otto Rank showed how great artists constantly reinvent their own mental frames of reference, stepping away from the established ways of doing things and finding new ways based on their own personal experience and observation. It was that ability to think beyond the confines of convention, outside of the box, that made them great.[12]

The ethical leader can learn a great deal from this approach. Reflecting on the decisions we have made and the outcomes they have generated, questioning how we do things and why, will help to enrich our thinking and broaden our minds to new possibilities. Pragmatically, this will make us better at exploring situations and generating options, but at a deeper level, it will assist our moral development. To paraphrase Confucius, the cultivation of virtue begins by looking inward and reflecting on ourselves.

The Markkula Center framework

The final model was developed at the Markkula Center for Applied Ethics at the University of Santa Clara in California. It too consists of a series of open questions, although there is also an app that requires users to input numerical scores. This, too my mind, is a bit too deterministic, and can lead to the app effectively making the decision for you, or at least, people being unwilling to go against the app scores even if they don't feel confident or comfortable with the decision. Students who have used the app largely agree, though some liked the feeling of certainty it appeared to give them.

THE MARKKULA CENTER FRAMEWORK

Recognize an ethical issue

1   Could this decision or situation be damaging to someone or to some group? Does this decision involve a choice between a good and bad alternative, or perhaps between two 'goods' or between two 'bads'?
2   Is this issue about more than what is legal or what is most efficient? If so, how?

Get the facts

1   What are the relevant facts of the case? What facts are not known? Can I learn more about the situation? Do I know enough to make a decision?
2   What individuals and groups have an important stake in the outcome? Are some concerns more important? Why?
3   What are the options for acting? Have all the relevant persons and groups been consulted? Have I identified creative options?

Evaluate alternative actions

1   Which option will produce the most good and do the least harm?
2   Which option best respects the rights of all who have a stake?
3   Which option treats people equally or proportionately?
4   Which option best serves the community as a whole, not just some members?
5   Which option leads me to act as the sort of person I want to be?

Make a decision and test it

1   Considering all these approaches, which option best addresses the situation?
2   If I told someone I respect – or told a television audience – which option I have chosen, what would they say?

Act and reflect on the outcome

1 How can my decision be implemented with the greatest care and
   attention to the concerns of all stakeholders?

2 How did my decision turn out and what have I learned from this
   specific situation?[13]

The Markkula framework is much more directly grounded in ethical theory than either Nash or Josephson. It refers explicitly to pragmatism, consequentialism and utilitarianism, as well as to virtue ethics and Rawls's theory of justice, and also to a couple of other theories we have not explored in this book, namely, the *rights approach* which argues that our primary duty as ethical beings is to respect the moral and physical rights of others, and the *common good approach*, which states that our ethical duty is to the community as a whole, not to individuals.[14]

Both are fairly simplistic in outlook, which is why I did not discuss them earlier in the book. Also, unlike the four approaches discussed in Chapter 2, neither is universal. Not every culture or philosophy recognizes the primacy of rights over responsibilities: Asian culture, indeed, tends to be the other way around, emphasizing community responsibility over individual rights. The same is true of the common good approach; Western cultures rooted in Enlightenment thinking will deny that the common good necessarily trumps the needs of the individual.

Recognize an ethical issue

1 Could this decision or situation be damaging to someone or to some
   group? Does this decision involve a choice between a good and bad
   alternative, or perhaps between two 'goods' or between two 'bads'?

2 Is this issue about more than what is legal or what is most efficient? If
   so, how?

The title of this section is curious because it suggests that there will be some issues that do not have ethical implications. In practice, given that virtually every decision we make has consequences for someone else, unintended or no, this is a meaningless distinction. In business, we need to consider the ethical implications of *every* decision we make. As noted above, the Markkula framework takes largely consequentialist, outcome-based view. In practice, deontological right-and-wrong issues will also be important, even if only in the form of compliance with legislation and regulation.

Get the facts

1   What are the relevant facts of the case? What facts are not known? Can I learn more about the situation? Do I know enough to make a decision?

2   What individuals and groups have an important stake in the outcome? Are some concerns more important? Why?

3   What are the options for acting? Have all the relevant persons and groups been consulted? Have I identified creative options?

As with the previous two frameworks, it is critically important to ensure that we have enough reliable information on which to make a decision. If the answer to 'do I know enough to make a decisions?' is no, then we have two choices: make a risky decision based on partial knowledge, or delay the decision until more knowledge becomes available, further studies have been carried out and so on.

Both options, to proceed or to wait, have ethical implications. This is reflected in questions 2 and 3. Who are the other actors in this scenario? Have we consulted them, or even identified all of them correctly? What will the consequences be for them if we take the risk? What will the outcome be if we delay? What are the rights and wrongs? What do we feel in our gut is the best thing to do?

Question 3 also nods to pragmatism and asks if we have created a sufficient number of viable options. Have we thought about the issue from different perspectives? Have we considered creative solutions rather than tried-and-tested formulae?

Evaluate alternative actions

1   Which option will produce the most good and do the least harm?

2   Which option best respects the rights of all who have a stake?

3   Which option treats people equally or proportionately?

4   Which option best serves the community as a whole, not just some members?

5   Which option leads me to act as the sort of person I want to be?

This is a simpler version of the Josephson Institute framework but, again, is more strongly grounded in different theories of ethics. With the Josephson framework, the door is open for us to pick and choose which issues we think are important. The Markkula framework closes that door and forces us to look at the implications from a variety of angles.

Which option will produce the most good and do the least harm is, of course, a consequentialist question. It adopts the utilitarian perspective of the greatest good for the greatest number, and accepts that in producing good for the many, there may well be harm for the few. This is, of course, a fairly broadly accepted principle in Western society. Democracy, for example, is founded on the idea of majority rule – the party or coalition with the most votes or the most seats forms the government.

The question then is, what happens to the minority who did not vote for that position? Does the majority party have a responsibility to govern on their behalf as well, seeking to accommodate their position? This was the philosophy of the Conservative Party in Britain from the 1950s to the 1980s, the so-called 'one-nation' policy in which it was assumed that no matter who held the reins of power, they had a responsibility to govern on behalf of everyone, not just the people who voted for them. Today, lip service is still paid to that philosophy, but it is rarely adhered to in practice. One of the least attractive outcomes of the Brexit referendum was the football analogy, employed by both sides, of win-lose. One side won absolutely, and all the other side can do is accept the result, lick their wounds and plot revenge. The idea that the two sides should work together to produce the best possible result for everyone is openly scorned.

This was what John Stuart Mill came to dislike about utilitarianism, and it is a real danger. Consider, for example, the revival of the trend for employee democracy, or at least workplace consultation. If we listen to our employees and then follow the majority view, what happens to the dissenting minority? If we simply ignore them, there is the real risk that dissent will fester and in time lead to non-compliance or even resistance. But also, there is an ethical dimension. The principle of fairness advocated by John Rawls says that it is wrong to simply govern on behalf of the majority. Ethics and good management practice dictate that we must try to take everyone with us. We will probably fail; but we must try, and we must be seen to be trying.

Which option best respects the rights of all who have a stake and *which option treats people equally or proportionately* are exactly the questions we must ask in order to address that issue. This must be done regardless of personal feeling. A community pressure group may be hurling inaccurate and unfair abuse at our organization, trying to drag our name through the mud, in order to advance its own agenda. Does this give us the right to take up a confrontational position, fight back, disregard this community and its wants? Again, good practice and ethical behaviour are in accord. Getting into dogfights with pressure groups is almost never a good idea; these are negative-sum conflicts where in the end everyone loses out, community and company alike. From an ethical point of view, we need to step around the mud and seek the higher moral ground. Do what is best for everyone, make it clear what you are doing and communicate your message clearly, and eventually people will understand you and come to see who you really are. Support for the pressure groups will gradually dry up.

If our attention is focused solely or primarily on the pursuit of profit, then it makes sense to take a pure utilitarian perspective and accept that some people will lose out. But creating collateral damage in this way is risky. Balancing the needs of all stakeholders, even those who don't like us, and treating them all fairly, not only reduces this risk but improves public perception of us and our actions.

Earlier in this book I mentioned the case of Tata Finance, the financial services company in the Tata Group that collapsed owing to very large debts. The managing director of Tata Finance was arrested and sent to prison, awaiting trial on various charges. Bringing complex cases to trial in India can take years, and the managing director applied for release on bail. The Tata Group opposed bail at first, but after a time it dropped its opposition, and the managing director was granted bail and freed. I asked Ratan Tata why Tata had changed its mind. 'Because it wasn't fair to him', came the response. 'He should face the judicial process and receive the appropriate punishment, but for him to sit in prison for years awaiting trial seemed wrong.' Fairness – even to people who have harmed you or damaged you. It is not an easy thing to do, but it is the right thing to do.

Which option best serves the community as a whole, not just some members brings us to the common good principle alluded to above. As mentioned, this is not always an easy principle to put into effect, especially in strongly individualistic societies where personal rights trump community needs, but it *is* important to remember those needs and to consider that perhaps communities have rights too.

And, finally, there is *which option leads me to act as the sort of person I want to be.* This question has its roots in virtue ethics, and I cannot stress its importance strongly enough. Personal feelings do matter. We can tick boxes in frameworks, fill in spreadsheets and weight and evaluate options until we are blue in the face, but ultimately, we must be personally comfortable with the decisions we make. If all the evidence points to one option but there is nagging whisper of doubt in your mind, listen to that whisper. It is telling you something the unconscious mind knows, but the conscious mind has not yet got around to figuring out.

Choose the option, not just that you can live with, but that you will be proud of. When mentoring or acting as a critical friend, I sometimes ask another question: *what would you like as your epitaph?* How would you like to sum up, not just your achievements, but the kind of person you are?

Make a decision and test it

1   Considering all these approaches, which option best addresses the situation?

2   If I told someone I respect – or told a television audience – which option I have chosen, what would they say?

Rather than the complicated decision section of the Josephson Institute framework, the Markkula framework assumes that by the time we reach the decision threshold we already have a fair idea of which decision is the best. Run over the options again, and then apply one final test, the sunlight test. The Markkula suggestion – would we be comfortable discussing our decision in front of a television audience – is a good one because, if things go wrong, there is a fair chance that we will be doing exactly that.

Act and reflect on the outcome

1   How can my decision be implemented with the greatest care and attention to the concerns of all stakeholders?

2   How did my decision turn out and what have I learned from this specific situation?

One of the weaknesses of the Nash framework is that it does not give enough attention to the consequences of action. The Markkula framework, like the Josephson framework, embraces the concept of action learning and urges us to constantly look back at the decisions we made, examine their consequences and learn from both successes and weaknesses.

The other important element here is attention to detail in implementation. It is a truism in management that many good decisions go wrong because of failures to implement them correctly, and that is true here as well. We need to not only make decisions based on ethical criteria, but also to implement them in an ethical manner.

Students who have used the framework like this aspect of it. They also like how the evaluation section draws on different theories to generate different perspectives. Otherwise, though, they find it, like the Nash framework, to be overly consequentialist and focus too much on outcomes and not enough on issues of right and wrong. If a thing is good, the Markkula approach seems to be saying, it must ipso facto also be right.

If you find any – or all – of these three frameworks useful, then go ahead and use them. From experience, I am aware that everyone's needs will be different, depending on their role and circumstances and also personal cognitive processes. Some people like frameworks and tools that give them quick outputs and are impatient with long processes, while others prefer a more methodical approach. Each of us approaches problem solving in different ways, and that is as it should be.

The Nash framework's strength is that it is quick to use, but it is better suited to relatively simple problems and lacks the depth to explore more complex dilemmas. Conversely, the Josephson Institute framework is good at teasing out detail, but it is lengthy and takes time to work through, and its use can sometimes equate to using a sledgehammer to crack a walnut. Neither is deeply grounded in ethical theory, which some might think is no bad thing; but I would argue that we need to remember those first principles of ethics discussed in Chapter 2, to make sure that we really are covering all the angles. The Markkula Center framework does this, but having given us a rounded evaluation tool it then rather surprisingly switches the focus back to consequentialist outcomes.

I am also aware that all three frameworks, even Nash, require people to stop, sit down and analyse problems in a methodical way. This is not always possible. As the Canadian strategy guru Henry Mintzberg has pointed out, conventional management theory assumes managers have the time and mental capacity to act rationally at all times. They receive information, evaluate it and then make decisions based on all available information in the manner of the frameworks described above.

Real life, says Mintzberg, is rather different. In his book *The Nature of Managerial Work*, he shows how managers spend most of their time 'fire-fighting', reacting to events, making quick decisions to solve the problem and then moving on to the next issue that confronts them.[15] In terms of information gathering, they sometimes have time to talk with a few friends and colleagues and mull over what is happening, but neither information gathering nor analysis is in any way systematic. Quite often, even this is not possible. The manager has to make a decision *now*, based only on what he or she already knows and what gut feeling is telling them. Mintzberg's study was done in the 1970s, but in the modern era of delayering and flat hierarchies, my observation is that this has become more true rather than less.

The Flat White framework

With this in mind, I have tried to come up with a simple framework for ethical decisions that is rooted in ethical theory and tries to cover all the bases but is also quick to use and requires no consultation. The admitted weakness of this framework is that it allows no time for gathering information, but as Mintzberg points out, we often don't have time to gather information anyway, so we have to 'go with what we've got'. If you have someone else to help you talk things over, well and good, but if necessary you can work through this framework on your own.

A little reflective time is required, but only a little. It should be possible to ask and answer these questions in about the same time as it takes to order and drink a flat white (other varieties of caffeinated drink are also available).

THE FLAT WHITE FRAMEWORK

1 What do we know about this situation, and what don't we know?
2 What are our own loyalties and biases? What might influence our decision one way or the other?
3 What stakeholder groups are involved, and how?
4 What options are open to us? If they are unsatisfactory, can other options be created?
5 What issues of right and wrong are involved?
6 What are the good and bad consequences of these options?
7 Which option would yield the result that is most fair and equitable?
8 What do you want to do?
9 In your heart, what do you feel you *should* do?
10 Can you live with the consequences of your actions?
11 What will you do if it turns out your decision is wrong?

Don't labour the process. Be quick and concise in your answers and try as far as possible to take a holistic view.

What do we know about this situation, and what don't we know? Sum up the key facts in a few sentences. Why is this issue important? What matters about it? What problems do we face? And, in the words of Donald Rumsfeld, what are the 'known unknowns'? Where do we lack information? If there is time to go and get it, do; if not, just be aware that this information void poses a risk as we go forward.

What are our own loyalties and biases? What might influence our decision one way or the other? We all like to think we are highly objective, but in truth none of us are, and even the most highly rigorous articles in the most prestigious scientific journals have a bias. We view the world through lenses that can sometimes – often? – distort our vision. Knowing what those lenses are helps us understand further the risks we run when making a decision. If we know ourselves well enough, there is usually no need to ask this question; we know the answer already.

The question of what influences can be brought to bear is a more tricky one. We may be under pressure from blackmailers to make a quick decision in their favour. The board of directors may similarly be exerting pressure to take a decision that favours certain shareholders.

Those kinds of influence are easy to see, but other factors are more subtle. Research has found that the physical environment of the workplace can have a strong impact on psychological well-being, and that in turn impacts on the decision we make.[16] If we work in a gloomy, depressing workplace we are more likely to be gloomy and depressed ourselves, and this can lead to a temptation to take the easy way out. A bright, friendly workplace produces greater confidence, and we are more likely to put our chins forward, take a brave pill and do the right thing.

Even something so small as the time of day can make a difference. In a fascinating article entitled 'The Morning Morality Effect', Maryam Kouchaki and Isaac Smith advance evidence to suggest that people are more likely to make ethical decisions early in the day, and that propensity to cut corners and take unethical decisions increases as the day goes on.[17] (And when do most boards of directors meet? In the afternoon …)

The point is beware of the subtle influences. As you drink your cup of coffee and mull things over, look around. Where are you? What time is it? What pressures are your environment exerting on you? If you don't like the vibe you feel in the air, move. Walk down the hallway, go outside, find a place where you can finish your coffee and think clearly.

What stakeholder groups are involved, and how? If we know our business well, then we already know the answer to this question. Spell it out in a few quick sentences, based on knowledge and experience.

What options are open to us? If they are unsatisfactory, can other options be created? This can be more tricky, because the pressures noted above can be inclining us towards a particular option already. We need to avoid being painted into a corner. We also need to avoid binary yes-no choices if at all possible. I suggest following the Josephson Institute framework here and generating at least three options. If that proves difficult, a second cup of coffee might be needed; if it is still impossible, seek advice from colleagues. Three options should be the minimum in all but the simplest of cases.

What issues of right and wrong are involved? There are legal issues, of course, but again, we should already be familiar with these. If we are not, mark this down under 'known unknowns' and seek advice. Beyond legality, there is also morality. What do right and wrong mean in this context? What does basic morality tell us we should do?

What are the good and bad consequences of these options? We can run through these with each involved stakeholder group, and again, if we know our stakeholders well, we should be able to tease out the key issues fairly quickly. What benefits will each group receive, and what externalities might they suffer? We should be able to list these in our heads, or write them down on the back of a napkin.

Which option would yield the result that is most fair and equitable? Of course, we have to ask ourselves, fair to whom? There is always a temptation to slip into utilitarianism here, but we need to remember Rawls's criteria:

1   every person has a right to liberty, but their freedom should never be allowed to impinge on the liberty of others

2   the least advantaged members of society should be protected as far as possible from social and economic inequalities

Rather than going for majority rule, think what result might be palatable to everyone.

What do you want to do? Having answered the questions above, which option makes the most sense? Which do you feel is the best choice? And then, having answered this, look inside yourself and ask, *in your heart, what do you feel you should do?* What is your instinct telling you to do? Which option makes you feel happy and releases oxytocin? Which ones make the hair stand up on your neck? If all three options produce the latter effect, time to think again.

Then, of course, there is the sunlight test, *can you live with the consequences of your actions?* and then the last and some way the most important question, *what will you do if it turns out your decision is wrong?* In part this is simple risk management, but there are deeper issues too. If we make a decision that we think is the right thing to do in the circumstances, and then as a result of that decision someone is injured or killed, then we have to live with that guilt. Some people can shrug these things off and get on with their lives, but I am not sure I want to know those people, let alone work with them. Most of us will feel trauma. And even less disastrous decisions can end up costing the company money and time, or result in unhappiness and harmful externalities to stakeholders.

And yet, mistakes will happen. We are only human, and as leaders we almost never have enough time and information to make fully informed and rational decisions. Risk is omnipresent. As the examples of Air France and Maple Leaf Foods show, the real test of an ethical leader is how they cope with failure. Because failure will come. The question is, are we ready for it when it knocks on the door?

If at the end of the process you are still confused and genuinely don't know what to do, then it is time to push the red button. Halt the process, shut things down, gather your team together and go through one of the more formal and detailed frameworks above. The cup of coffee framework will work perhaps

60 per cent of the time, but don't force the issue. The most important rule of ethical decision making is this:

Never, ever take a decision which leaves you feeling unhappy or which you know in your heart is wrong.

Decision making and risk

To repeat, even if we are happy with the decision at the time, circumstances change. A decision which was right when it was made can go disastrously wrong a few years or even a few months later.

One complaint about the ethical decision-making frameworks given above, and indeed about all such frameworks, is that they can be constrictive. When considering the ethical implications of our decisions, we can become so frightened of the risks that we withdraw into our shells and do nothing.

Sometimes, doing nothing is the right thing to do. The old adage that 'it is better to do the wrong thing than nothing at all' is nonsense. Sometimes, as the Daoists point out, purposeful non-action, laissez-faire, is the best course. Watch and wait can be a very useful strategy.[18] But not always.

In his book *On the Psychology of Military Incompetence*, Norman Dixon talks about how fear of doing the wrong thing can paralyse us into inaction. He uses the example of the Royal Navy, where it is standard procedure for captains who lose their ships, either in battle or shipwreck, to face a court-martial. The purpose of the court is to inquire into the circumstances of the ship's sinking, but captains see the court as a judgement on themselves and their own effectiveness. They become so frightened of losing their ship and facing a court-martial that they become risk-averse and refuse to put their ships into danger. And yet, in wartime, during storms, in search and rescue operations, the captain's duty is very often precisely that, to hazard the ship in order to carry out their duty.[19]

So it is with all leaders. We face risk every day, and we must not back down from it. Ethical leaders seek to make decisions that will *reduce* risk, but they do not seek to avoid it. That in itself would be unethical. Decision-making frameworks are not shields. We cannot use them to hide from risk. Instead, we should see them as enablers, tools that help us face the future with confidence knowing we have made the best possible decision in the circumstances.

11

If Not Now, When?

I said at the beginning that this book was all about making money. As will have become evident by now, I lied. I leave it to you to decide whether it was unethical of me to do so.

Actually, on one level I was telling the truth. What this book is *really* about is creating value, and, if you can create value efficiently and effectively with a minimum of externalities, then like I said, you really will make money. But that is the beginning of the story, not the end.

Like Kenichi Ohmae, whom I mentioned in Chapter 2, the strategy guru Henry Mintzberg argues that thinking about strategy is something that should be part of everyday managerial work, rather than a separate process.[1] He talks about 'crafting' strategy, letting it evolve naturally rather than trying to force the process. In this book, I have tried to take a similar approach to ethics. Rather than treating ethics as some sort of separate process, distinct from other business activities, we need to train ourselves to think of ethics as something that is intrinsic to everything we do. Every decision we make has ethical implications, and we need to consider those at every stage of the process.

We should do so, of course, not just for reasons of enlightened self-interest but because this is the way business should be done. Thinking about our stakeholders and treating them ethically, shouldering the burden of responsibility for our actions, building relationships of trust with customers and employees and communities: these all make good business sense. As I showed in Chapters 4 and 5, businesses like Tata, McKinsey and John Lewis have built these ideas into their business model: trust and responsibility and service.

But, as I hope this book makes plain, there is more to it than that. Deontology tells us the rules, consequentialism helps us to assess outcomes and pragmatism opens the doors to multiple solutions. But a dash of good old Aristotelian virtue ethics is needed too. Ultimately, as I have said several times in this book, we need to be the people we want to be. We need to be proud of our decisions and our achievements, so that when the time comes to shuffle off this mortal coil, we can say hand on heart that we did our best for everyone who depended on us, and that we are leaving the world a slightly better place than when we found it.

During the course of my research into the Tata Group I interviewed one of the group's grand old men, R.K. Krishna Kumar. When I met him he was head of Tata Global Beverages, but he had been involved with many companies in the group over the years.

I asked him, as I asked everyone, what he thought the values of the Tata brand were. He did not answer immediately. Instead he gazed out the window for a while, steepling his fingers, and it was perhaps five seconds or so before he spoke. 'What you must realise', he said, 'is that this is not a brand story. This is a story about good and evil.'

I was dumbstruck. I had asked a question about marketing; why were we suddenly discussing metaphysics? I also admit I was a little uncomfortable. I am an ordinary cynical agnostic Canadian; I don't tend to have conversations about good and evil, and find them rather emotive subjects. But I listened while R.K. Krishna Kumar explained his philosophy, and I began to understand.

The world, he said (and I am paraphrasing heavily here), is full of bad things. War, hunger, sickness, poverty, illiteracy, refugees fleeing persecution, destitute people trying and often failing to hold their lives together; those things, he said, can fairly be called evil. If we accept this, then we as business leaders have two choices. We can turn our back, in which case we become part of the problem. Or we can use the very limited power we have to try and make a difference, to alleviate at least some of the problems we see around us. And if we do so, then we can with fairness be called good.

The choice is ours. Which do we want to be? Part of the problem, or part of the solution? If you are still reading this book, then I am guessing it is the latter (if you wanted to be part of the problem, you would have thrown the book away by now).

So, what next? In this book, we have discussed what ethics is and what ethical leaders do, the processes of value creation and the ethical value chain, and some frameworks and tools for embedding ethics in decision making. Those are the building blocks; what you do with them is up to you.

Appendix 1:
Ethical Dilemmas for
Practice

Below are six dilemmas that you can use for practice using the ethical decision-making frameworks outlined in Chapter 10. Some are quite simple and involve low-level team and personal issues. Others are more complex and affect the entire organization. All require you to make a moral as well as a purely economic or business choice. All these dilemmas are real, but like the Blackley shipyard case they have been heavily disguised to ensure the people and companies mentioned remain anonymous.

Pick a framework you like and use it to analyse the dilemmas that interest you most. If you have time, try using more than one framework to see if you get a different response. In MBA classes, I divide student into six groups, giving each a different dilemma along with all four frameworks. I invite them to analyse their dilemma using all the frameworks, and then tell the rest of the room what decisions they reached and why. This could, if you wish, be a useful group exercise. Alternatively, it can something simple that you do yourself.

As noted in Chapter 11, practice is important. Get used to thinking about decisions in an ethical light, so that it becomes second nature to you. If you can think ethically without even realizing you are doing so, then you have become an ethical leader.

The leak

About two years ago, the investment bank for which you work hired a banker named Edward. Edward had twice previously been investigated on suspicion of passing insider information about his clients to other firms. However, both investigations cleared him fully, and in one case it was discovered that the insider information had actually been passed on by another member of Edward's team without his knowledge.

Despite being officially cleared, some members of your bank were not happy about hiring Edward, believing he had a dubious reputation. Others, including the board, were inclined to give him the benefit of the doubt and pointed out that there was no evidence against him. Edward, however, did not stay long with your bank but moved on after about eighteen months to a rival bank, Redstone.

For some time, your team had been advising a British manufacturing firm, Dudley Enterprises. Dudley makes solar generation equipment, and has patents on some revolutionary new technologies which have the potential to nearly double energy outputs from solar panels (through a combination of more efficient capacitors and cables and batteries which reduce energy 'spillage').

Earlier in the year, a couple of months before Edward's departure, Dudley received an offer from a German company, DMK, which was being advised by Redstone (the bank where Edward now works). The German firm offered to buy Dudley Enterprises at a price of £14 per share. The directors of Dudley Enterprises were inclined to accept the offer; they wanted the additional investment DMK could offer in order to develop their product and bring it to market. But your team advised them that the firm and its technology were worth much more than this, and recommended Dudley hold out for at least £23 a share. The directors agreed to hold firm. But a week later, DMK made a further offer of £15 per share and the directors accepted it against your advice.

Your bosses were not happy about this, as the bank lost a sizeable sum in commissions thanks to the lower price. However, the deal appeared to be above board and both Dudley Enterprises and DMK were very happy with the deal, the latter promising to invest more in Dudley Enterprises and create jobs. Then, a chance conversation with a banker at Redstone revealed that his bank knew that Dudley Enterprises were willing to settle for a lower price, and advised DMK accordingly.

Your first thought was that one of the directors of Dudley Enterprises may have leaked the information, but the person from Redstone was positive that this was not the case. That means the information must have leaked from your own bank, and Edward is the most likely culprit. If he did learn this information and pass it on, then he is guilty of insider trading, which is a criminal offence. Your duty is to report this matter to the regulator. However, you have no proof; both parties in the deal are happy with it; and if you blow the whistle and accuse Edward of wrongdoing, your bosses may not be happy about your making waves. It is even possible that you yourself could be accused of passing on the information to Redstone.

Bob

You are a director of a steel making company with several plants in the UK. Bob, your head of health and safety, who reports to you, is a veteran of the industry, having worked in steel for more than thirty years. He is one of the best health and safety experts in the entire industry, and your firm went to a great deal of effort to hire him away from a rival company several years ago, in an effort to improve your own health and safety record.

Bob was given the task of leading the transformation of the health and safety environment and bringing about a complete culture change through the company. The aim is to reach a 'zero harm' environment where accidents of any kind are not tolerated and are prevented. The policy has full buy-in at board level, and the chairman and CEO are in full support. It is up to Bob, however, to design and implement the new policy and to give the lead on how and where the culture needs to change.

Bob is charismatic, well liked and respected by the men who work on the floor of the steel mills. It is clear that they are listening to him and accepting his message about the need to change. However, lately his behaviour has become somewhat erratic. He has missed several meetings without explanation, and he often looks very tired. A month ago, you spoke to him about this and urged him to take a holiday, but he refused to do so, citing a heavy workload. Then, in a casual conversation with him a week later, you thought you smelled alcohol on his breath. You noticed this again several days later, and asked Bob if he had been drinking while on the job.

This is a serious matter, for the firm's own health and safety regulations ban anyone from drinking while or shortly before working on the floor of a steel mill, and Bob regularly visits these mills to inspect conditions. Bob himself has made it clear that there must be zero tolerance for alcohol impairment while at work.

When you asked him the question as to whether he had been drinking, Bob grew angry and denied this, telling you that you had insulted his professionalism and threatening to quit if you ever raised the allegation again. What do you do next?

Majority rule?

You are the managing director of British Dairy Cooperatives (BDC), an agricultural co-operative of dairy farmers who supply milk to a variety of UK customers, including supermarkets, industrial makers of cheese, butter and infant formula (milk for small babies). You have about 600 members across the country, who are the effective owners of the business; each has an equal say and an equal vote in how the business is run.

As managing director, your duties include running the co-operative on a day-to-day basis, negotiating prices and delivery terms with customers, but also ensuring that BDC's very high-quality standards are respected and enforced. BDC is not an organic producer, but it does have a reputation for high quality, especially in terms of food safety. Milking parlours, tankers and processing plants are cleaned thoroughly and rigorously inspected, with a thorough system of testing. This means that your milk products are slightly more expensive, but so far customers have respected this and been willing to pay a premium.

BDC has always very strongly about environmental ethics, about respecting the natural environment and particularly the cows that produce the milk. The co-operative also felt that it had a responsibility to its customers and the end consumers, to deliver a product that was as safe as it could possibly be. There is amongst some members, at least, an inherent belief in the 'goodness' of milk, and that there is a responsibility to protect consumers from contamination and provide nourishing food. This is particularly true of the milk supplied for infant formula, where even slight contamination can be life-threatening.

Last month, two of your main customers asked for a price reduction. They have cited falling milk prices driven by the availability of higher quantities of imported milk. The co-operative argued that much of the imported milk is not as rigorously controlled and tested, and therefore carries a potential health risk. The customers disagreed, insisting on the price reduction and threatening to move to another supplier if you do not comply. This is a serious matter, and by the terms of the co-operative's constitution, all members must vote on any price change. To your astonishment, a bare majority (54 per cent) voted for the price reduction, recommending that it be paid for by scrapping part of the cleaning and inspection system and going back to the basic level of food safety regulation required by law. They claimed that BDC's additional measures were unnecessary and were making the co-operative uncompetitive.

However, the remaining 46 per cent of members were angered by this. Some have threatened that if the price reduction goes through, they will leave the co-operative. If they do, the business itself might no longer be able to meet is current contracts. Their opponents have pointed out that they have a majority, and that their will should be respected; if it is not, then they too might choose to leave.

As managing director, you are required to negotiate a compromise that will satisfy both parties. How can you do so in a way that does not compromise BDC's ethics?

The hard choice

You are head of a small team in a large publishing company, responsible for publishing books. There are five people in your team, all with the same duties; they are responsible for finding authors for books, arranging contracts and the liaising with the author and the production team (typesetter, copy editor and proof reader) through to publication. All five members of your team have good skills sets and all perform well.

The board has recently announced a restructuring of the company, with more of its operations to be outsourced to contract editorial service providers who have superior networks and lower costs, and can do the same work to the same standard but more cheaply. This means that in-house teams will have to shrink. Your own boss has informed you that you will have to make one of your team members redundant. There is no choice in the matter; this must be done. There is a small redundancy package, equivalent to three months' pay, but no other benefits are on offer.

Martha, aged 40, is the oldest member of the team. She has been working in publishing for many years for very low wages compared to elsewhere in business, but she loves her job. She is very good at what she does, but her skills set is quite narrow. She has no work experience outside of publishing, and would struggle to find work anywhere except in publishing. Unfortunately, most publishers are in the same position as your own and are letting people go. No new jobs are being created.

Tom, aged 25, is a relatively new recruit who joined straight after his undergraduate degree. He was seen as a potential high-flyer when he first joined, someone who could do very well in the business. However, being young and not long in the business, he still has relatively little experience. He is married; his wife is a full-time mother who looks after their two small children, and so the family are dependent on Tom's salary. Last year, Tom was involved in a road accident which left him wheelchair-bound. He insisted on coming back to work early, against the advice of his doctors, and there is no doubting his enthusiasm for his job.

John, aged 30, is a very hard-working dependable person, in many ways the backbone of the team. If the others are ever in difficulty, they know they can turn to John and he will help them, with personal as well as professional problems. Losing John would be a real blow to team morale. He is single with no dependents. Before moving into the publishing industry he worked in advertising and still has some contacts there.

Julie, aged 32, is quiet but very capable. She has excellent relationships with her authors, many of whom publish with your company only because of her. She is single. Her mother has early-onset dementia, very severely, and requires twenty-four-hour nursing care. Julie depends on her job for the money to pay for nursing care, which consumes nearly all of her salary. She too has spent her entire working career in publishing and would struggle to find work elsewhere.

David is 28 and married with three children. He too has a mortgage and struggles to get by on an editor's salary. He has often spoken of making a change, doing something else with his life, but he has a bachelor's degree in

English literature and is not certain what else he would be suited for. David is also an instinctively gifted editor who can almost 'smell' a good book that will appeal to readers. Last year, his books accounted for a third of all the revenues earned by the team's books.

One of these five must be made redundant – but which one? There is, of course, the standard rule of last in–first out, which would point to Tom. But is that the best decision for the people involved? Is that the best decision for the business?

Between a rock and a hard place

You are the managing director of a tea growing and importing firm headquartered in London but owning extensive estates in northeast India, in the Himalayan foothills. You visit India frequently to inspect operations there and sort out problems.

The hills near your plantations are also home to a Maoist guerrilla movement called the Shining Light. This movement has about 5,000 well-armed and determined fighters, and so far the Indian security forces have been unable to touch them. A year ago, Shining Light guerrillas raided several of your plantations. Buildings were burned and machinery smashed, and over £100,000 of damage was done. Worse, four of your workers were killed and two managers were taken hostage and released only after your company agreed to pay a £20,000 ransom.

You appealed to both the state and national governments in India, but to no avail. Resources are stretched thin, and the government cannot spare any men to guard your plantations.

Your local managers suggested that you negotiate with the guerrillas. Several other tea companies have done the same in the past, with success. After consulting your directors you decided to follow this path. Using an intermediary, you negotiated a truce with the guerrillas on condition that you pay them £5,000 a month. This is not excessive and your company can afford it. A deal was reached, and you have been paying the Shining Light for several months, during which time your plantations have not been attacked or threatened. All appears to be going well.

Last week, the Indian government informed you that it had found out about this arrangement. You have been ordered to cease all payments at once, otherwise your local managers will be arrested and charged with aiding a terrorist organization. This is a very serious offence and carries with it a lengthy prison sentence. Your company will also be prosecuted and fined. Finally, you yourself will be arrested on your next visit to India and likewise charged with aiding terrorists, unless the payments cease immediately.

What will you do?

Hunger games

You are an official with a charity working to deliver aid to starving people in rural Somalia. At the time of this dilemma, Somalia has no effective government and has effectively been divided up by a number of local warlords, each controlling their own territory. There is no functioning market economy, and aid delivered by charities on behalf of international aid organizations is the only source of food that many people have.

You are in charge of a convoy of trucks taking aid to an impoverished district where the food situation has become critical. People are starving, and, if your convoy does not get through, it is likely that some will begin to die. Shortly before you reach the district, your convoy encounters a roadblock manned by armed soldiers. These are local militiamen, loyal to one of the warlords. They tell you that you will not be allowed to proceed past the roadblock unless you hand over a sum of money, equivalent to about $10,000.

You can get the money; all you have to do is radio your headquarters in the capital, Mogadishu, and the money can be sent to you by car. However, you know that this particular warlord is aggressively expanding his territory at the expense of his neighbours. It seems certain that the money will be spent to buy arms and ammunition, which will be used to spread war and kill people.

On the other hand, if the convoy does not get through, then, as stated above, it is likely that people in the district will begin to die of starvation. Your decision is simple: do you pay off the bandits, knowing this could lead to people being killed in renewed fighting? Or do you refuse to pay and return your convoy to Mogadishu, leaving the starving people of the district to fend for themselves?

NOTES

Chapter 1

1   Luke Johnson, 'Lies, Damned Lies and Running a Business', *Financial Times*, http://www.ft.com/cms/s/0/364f2924-47e1-11e4-ac9f-00144feab7de.html#axzz3FH4CKRWx, 30 September 2014.

2   *The Guardian*, 'Uber CEO Travis Kalanick resigns following months of chaos', 20 June 2017, https://www.theguardian.com/technology/2017/jun/20/uber-ceo-travis-kalanick-resigns.

3   Ibid.

4   *The Guardian*, 'Uber executive fired amid reports he obtained rape victim's medical records', 7 June 2017, https://www.theguardian.com/technology/2017/jun/07/uber-executive-fired-eric-alexander-rape-case-india.

5   *New York Times*, 'Uber faces Federal inquiry over Greyball tool to evade authorities', 4 May 2017, https://www.nytimes.com/2017/05/04/technology/uber-federal-inquiry-software-greyball.html.

6   Ibid.

7   Lionel Robbins, *An Essay on the Nature and Significance of Economic Science*, London: Macmillan, 1935; Milton Friedman, *Capitalism and Freedom*, Chicago: University of Chicago Press, 1992.

8   Steven D. Levitt and Stephen J. Dubner, *Freakonomics*, New York: William Morrow, 2005.

9   Ray Monk, *Robert Oppenheimer: A Life Inside the Center*, New York: Doubleday, 2012, p. 467.

10 Henry Greely, *The Code of Codes: Scientific and Social Issues in the Human Genome Project*, Cambridge, MA: Harvard University Press, 1992.

11 Amartya Sen, *On Ethics and Economics*, Oxford: Blackwell.

12 https://www.cbsnews.com/news/mark-zuckerberg-facebook-ceo-cambridge-analytica-data-scandal-statement-today-2018-03-21/, 21 March 2018.

13 Ibid.

14 Ibid.

15 *New York Times*, 21 March 2018, 'Mark Zuckerberg Q and A', https://www.nytimes. com/2018/03/21/technology/mark-zuckerberg-q-and-a.html.

16 *Washington Post*, 'Germany tells social media companies to erase hate', 30 June 2017, https://www.washingtonpost.com/news/worldviews/wp/2017/06/30/with-new-law-germany-tells-social-media-companies-to-erase-hate-or-face-fines-up-to-57-million/?noredirect=on&utm_term=.9f296b4137cd.

17 *Bloomberg*, 'Weinstein Company files for Chapter 11 bankruptcy in Delaware court', 20 March 2018, https://www.bloomberg.com/news/articles/2018-03-20/weinstein-co-files-for-chapter-11-bankruptcy-in-delaware-court.

18 Ibid.

19 Reuters, 'Weinstein Company files for bankruptcy', 20 March 2018, https://www. reuters.com/article/us-weinstein-company-bankruptcy/the-weinstein-company-files-for-bankruptcy-idUSKBN1GW08P.

20 Morgen Witzel, *Managing for Success*, London: Bloomsbury, 2016.

21 *The Guardian*, 'Hotpoint tells customers to check fridge-freezers after Grenfell Tower fire', 23 June 2017, https://www.theguardian.com/uk-news/2017/jun/23/hotpoint-tells-customers-to-check-fridge-freezers-after-grenfell-tower-fire.

22 *The Times*, 'Minister orders Oxfam to hand over files on Haiti prostitute scandal', 9 February 2018, https://www.thetimes.co.uk/article/top-oxfam-staff-paid-haiti-quake-survivors-for-sex-mhm6mpmgw.

23 BBC, 'Oxfam Haiti scandal: Thousands cancel donations to charity', 20 February 2018, http://www.bbc.co.uk/news/uk-43121833.

24 BBC, 'Attacks are out of proportion, says Oxfam's Mark Goldring', 17 February 2018, http://www.bbc.co.uk/news/uk-politics-43095679.

25 Reuters, 'Sex scandals and Brexit lower Britain's global charity ranking', 30 April 2018, https://www.reuters.com/article/us-britain-charity-philanthropy/sex-scandals-and-brexit-lower-britains-global-charity-ranking-idUSKBN1I11X2.

26 Reuters, 'Cricket Australia slaps 12 month ban on Smith and Warner', 26 March 2018, https://www.reuters.com/article/us-cricket-test-zaf-aus-tampering/cricket-australia-slaps-12-month-bans-on-smith-and-warner-idUSKBN1H41ES.

27 Ibid.

28 CNN, 'Australia cricket scandal sponsors', 27 March 2018, http://money.cnn. com/2018/03/27/news/australia-cricket-scandal-sponsors/index.html.

29 Gay Haskins and Mike Thomas, 'Kindness and Its Many Manifestations', in Gay Haskins, Mike Thomas and Lalit Johri (eds), *Kindness in Leadership*, London: Routledge, 2018.

Chapter 2

1 Alasdair Macintyre, *A Short History of Ethics: A History of Moral Philosophy from the Homeric Age to the Twentieth Century*, London: Routledge, 1998; Steven M. Cahn and Peter Markie, *Ethics: History, Theory and Contemporary Issues*, Oxford: Oxford University Press, 1998; Michael Slote (ed.), *Essays on the History of Ethics*, Oxford: Oxford University Press, 2010.

2 Laozi, *Daodejing*, trans. John. C.H. Wu, London: Shambhala, 1990.

3 *The Guardian*, 'Up to 13,000 working as slaves in the UK', 29 November 2014, https://www.theguardian.com/world/2014/nov/29/13000-slaves-uk-four-times-higher-previously-thought; *Washington Post*, 'This map shows where the world's 30 million slaves live', 17 November 2013, https://www.washingtonpost.com/news/worldviews/wp/2013/10/17/this-map-shows-where-the-worlds-30-million-slaves-live-there-are-60000-in-the-u-s/?utm_term=.6d3731eba725.

4 Ronald Segal, *The Black Diaspora*, New York: Farrar, Strauss and Giroux, 1995.

5 Charles Fried, *Right and Wrong*, Cambridge, MA: Harvard University Press, 1978.

6 Immanuel Kant, *Groundwork of the Metaphysics of Morals*, New York: Harper & Row, 1964; Allan W. Wood, 'Kant's History of Ethics', *Studies in the History of Ethics*, June 2005, http://www.historyofethics.org/062005/062005Wood.shtml.

7 A.C. Prabhupada Bhaktivedante Swami (ed. and trans.) *Bhagavad-Gita As It Is*, New York: Collier, 1972.

8 Burton Watson, *Han Fei Tzu: Basic Writings*, New York: Columbia University Press, 1964; Morgen Witzel, 'The Leadership Philosophy of Han Fei', *Asia Pacific Business Review*, 18 (4), 2012, pp. 1–15.

9 Watson, *Han Fei Tzu*, p. 32.

10 W.D. Ross, *The Right and the Good*, Oxford: Clarendon, 1930.

11 John Rawls, *A Theory of Justice*, New York: Belknap, 1971.

12 Chen Huan-Chang, *The Economic Principles of Confucius and His School*, New York: Longmans, Green, 1911.

13 Jeremy Bentham, *An Introduction to the Principles of Morals and Legislation*, 1789; John Stuart Mill, *Utilitarianism*, 1861; Jonathan Glover (ed.), *Utilitarianism and Its Critics*, New York: Macmillan, 1990.

14 Jennifer Board, 'The Paradox of Ethics', in Richard Bolden, Morgen Witzel and Nigel Linacre (eds), *Leadership Paradoxes*, London: Routledge, 2016.

15 John Dewey, *Lectures on Ethics*, 1901; William James, *Pragmatism: A New Name for Some Old Ways of Thinking*, New York: Longmans, Green, 1907.

16 Alan D. Hertzke and Chris McRorie, 'The Concept of Moral Ecology', in Peter Lawler and Dale McConkey (eds), *Community and Political Thought Today*, Westport, CT: Praeger, 1998.

17 Ajit Nayak, 'Wisdom and the Tragic Question: Moral Learning and Emotional Perception in Leadership and Organisations', *Journal of Business Ethics*, 137, 2016, pp. 1–13.

18 Ibid., p. 1.

19 Roger Crisp, *Aristotle: Nicomachean Ethics*, Cambridge: Cambridge University Press, 2000; Burton Watson, *The Analects of Confucius*, New York: Columbia University Press, 2007.

20 Haskins et al., *Kindness in Leadership*, p. 15.

21 Paul J. Zak, 'Neuronomics', *Philosophical Transactions of the Royal Society, B: Biological Sciences*, 359, 2004, pp. 1737–48; Paul J. Zak, *The Moral Molecule: The Source of Love and Prosperity*, New York: Dutton, 2012.

22 Peter J. Buirski et al., 'Sex Differences, Dominance and Personality in the Chimpanzee', *Animal Behaviour*, 26 (1), 1978, pp. 123–9.

23 Morgen Witzel, *Tata: The Evolution of a Corporate Brand*, New Delhi: Penguin India, 2008.

24 Richard Bolden, Morgen Witzel and Nigel Linacre (eds), *Leadership Paradoxes*, London: Routledge, 2016.

25 Kenichi Ohmae, *The Mind of the Strategist*, New York: McGraw-Hill, 1982.

Chapter 3

1 Richard Bolden et al., *Exploring Leadership: Individual, Organizational and Societal Perspectives*, Oxford: Oxford University Press, 2011.

2 John P. Kotter, *Leading Change*, Boston: Harvard Business School Press, 1996.

3 Thomas North Whitehead, *Leadership in a Free Society*, London: Oxford University Press, 1936, p. 30.

4 Marco R. Furtner, Thomas Maran and John F. Rauthman, 'Dark Leadership: The Role of Leaders' Dark Triad Personality Traits', in Matthew G. Clark and Craig W. Gruber (eds), *Leadership Development Deconstructed*, New York: Springer, 2017, pp. 75–99.

5 Christian J. Resick et al., 'A Cross-Cultural Examination of the Endorsement of Ethical Leadership', *Journal of Business Ethics*, 63, 2006, p. 346.

6   John P. Kotter, *A Force for Change: How Leadership Differs from Management*, New York: The Free Press, 1990.

7   Leo Tolstoy, *War and Peace*, trans. Rosemary Edmonds, London: Penguin, 1957.

8   Mary Parker Follett, *Creative Experience*, New York: Longmans, Green, 1924.

9   John Lawlor and Jeff Gold, 'The Fog of Leadership', in Richard Bolden, Morgen Witzel and Nigel Linacre (eds), *Leadership Paradoxes*, London: Routledge, 2016.

10 Diane Perpich, *The Ethics of Emmanuel Levinas*, Stanford, CA: Stanford University Press, 2008.

11 Witzel, *Managing for Success*.

12 Theodore Levitt, 'Marketing Myopia', *Harvard Business Review*, 1960, https://hbr. org/2004/07/marketing-myopia.

13 Gerry Brown, *The Independent Director*, Basingstoke: Palgrave Macmillan, 2016.

14 Quoted in Chen, *The Economic Principles of Confucius and His School*.

15 Ibn Khaldun, *The Muqaddimah*, trans. Franz Rosenthal, London: Routledge, 1986; Raymond De Roover, 'Scholastic Economics: Survival and Lasting Influence from the Sixteenth Century to Adam Smith', *Quarterly Journal of Economics*, 69 (2), 1955, pp. 161–90, repr. in Mark Blaug (ed.), *St Thomas Aquinas*, Aldershot: Edward Elgar, 1991, pp. 67–96; Gene W. Heck, *Islam Inc.: An Early Business History*, Riyadh: King Faisal Center for Research and Islamic Studies, 2004.

16 Adam Smith, *The Theory of Moral Sentiments*, Edinburgh, 1759, repr. London: Forgotten Books, 2010.

17 Arthur Lowes-Dickinson, 'The necessity for greater publicity in management accounts', Rowntree Management Conference lecture, 25 September 1924.

18 E.C.G. England, 'The eternal quest', Rowntree Management Conference lecture, 30 September 1928.

19 John Lee, 'The Ethics of Industry', Rowntree Management Conference lecture, 23 September 1923.

20 Oliver Sheldon, *The Philosophy of Management*, London: Pitman, 1923.

21 Lyndall Fownes Urwick, *Management of Tomorrow*, London: Nisbet, 1933, p. 201.

22 Georges Duhamel, *Scènes de la vie future* (Pictures of Life in the Future), Paris: Éditions Mercure, 1928.

23 Edward Cadbury, *Experiments in Industrial Organization*, London: Longmans, Green, 1912.

24 John Spedan Lewis, *Fairer Shares*, London: Staples Press, 1954, p. 44.

25 W.K.K. Chan, 'The Organizational Structure of the Traditional Chinese Firm and Its Modern Reform', *Business History Review*, 56 (2), 1982, pp. 218–35; repr. in R. Ampalavanar Brown (ed.), *Chinese Business Enterprise: Critical Perspectives on Business and Management*, vol. 1, London: Routledge, 1982, pp. 216–30.

26 Witzel, *Tata*.

27 Tata Code of Conduct, p. 17, http://www.tata.com/pdf/tcoc-booklet-2015.pdf.

28 *The Guardian*, 'Staff ownership ensures organic veg firm Riverford doesn't forget its roots', 7 April 2018, https://www.theguardian.com/business/2018/apr/07/riverford-organic-veg-employee-ownership-plan.

29 BBC Radio 4, https://www.bbc.co.uk/programmes/b09ycftz.

30 Ricardo Semler, *Maverick*, New York: Warner Books, 1993.

31 *The Independent*, 'John Lewis is not up for sale, says chairman', 13 August 1999, https://www.independent.co.uk/news/business/john-lewis-is-not-up-for-sale-says-chairman-1112612.html.

Chapter 4

1 Witzel, *Tata*.

2 ABC News, 'Chic-fil-A backlash: Politicians, muppets respond', https://abcnews.go.com/WNT/video/chick-fil-backlash-politicians-muppets-respond-16857916.

3 Robert C. Alberts, *The Good Provider: H.J. Heinz and His 57 Varieties*, London: Arthur Barker, 1973, p. 57.

4 Peter Chapman, *The Last of the Imperious Rich*, London: Portfolio Penguin, 2010; Witzel, *Managing for Success*, chapter 3.

5 Chapman, *The Last of the Imperious Rich*, p. 200.

6 See Jared Dillan's later account, *Street Freak: Money and Madness at Lehman Brothers*, New York: Simon & Schuster, 2011.

7 Mary Jo Hatch and Majken Schultz, *Taking Brand Initiative: How Companies Can Align Strategy, Culture and Identity Through Corporate Branding*, Chichester: John Wiley, 2008.

8 *New York Post*, 'Self-employment is a rising trend in the American workforce', 25 March 2018, https://nypost.com/2018/03/25/self-employment-is-a-rising-trend-in-the-american-workforce/.

9 https://www.inc.com/articles/2000/11/14278.html.

10 Vineet Nayar, *Employees First, Customers Second: Turning Conventional Management Upside Down*, Boston: Harvard Business School Press, 2010.

11 Witzel, *Tata*, ch. 7.

12 *The Guardian*, 'Revealed: How Sports Direct effectively pays below the minimum wage', 9 December 2015, https://www.theguardian.com/business/2015/dec/09/how-sports-direct-effectively-pays-below-minimum-wage-pay.

13 *The Independent*, 'The 7 most shocking testimonies from workers at Sports Direct', 22 July 2016, https://www.independent.co.uk/news/business/news/sports-direct-mike-ashley-worker-conditions-minimum-wage-ian-wright-investigation-a7149971.html.

14 *Personnel Today*, 'Company directors face criminal charges over redundancies', 21 October 2015, https://www.personneltoday.com/hr/company-directors-face-criminal-charges-over-redundancy-consultation-rules/.

15 Masaaki Imai, *Kaizen: The Key to Japan's Competitive Success*, New York: Random House, 1996.

16 Navi Radjou, Jaideep Prabu and Simone Ahuja, *Jugaad Innovation: Think Frugal, Be Flexible, Generate Breakthrough Growth*, Chichester: Wiley, 2012.

17 Cadbury, *Experiments in Industrial Organization*.

18 Louis Gerstner, *Who Says Elephants Can't Dance? Leading a Great Enterprise Through Dramatic Change*, New York: HarperCollins, 2002; Peter E. Greulich, *A View from Beneath the Dancing Elephant: Rediscovering IBM's Corporate Constitution*, New York: MBI Concepts, 2014.

19 W. Chan Kim and Renée Mauborgne, *Blue Ocean Strategy: How to Create Uncontested Market Space and Make the Competition Irrelevant*, Boston: Harvard Business School Press, 2005; Patrick Barwise and Seán Meehan, *Beyond the Familiar: Long-Term Growth Through Customer Focus and Innovation*, San Francisco, CA: Jossey-Bass, 2011.

20 Joanna Barsh, Marla M. Capozzi and Jonathan Davidson, 'Leadership and Innovation', *McKinsey Quarterly*, January 2008, https://www.mckinsey.com/business-functions/strategy-and-corporate-finance/our-insights/leadership-and-innovation.

21 Unilever 2017 full year results, https://www.unilever.com/Images/ir-q4-2017-full-announcement_tcm244-515314_en.pdf.

22 John E.G. Bateson, *Managing Services Marketing*, Chicago: Dryden, 1998; Valarie Zeithaml, *Driving Customer Equity: How Customer Lifetime Value Is Reshaping Corporate Strategy*, Boston: Harvard Business School Press, 2007.

23 Judy Kuszewski, 'Case Study: IBM Smarter Planet', *Ethical Corporation*, 27 May 2013, http://www.ethicalcorp.com/business-strategy/case-study-ibm-smarter-planet.

24 *The Guardian*, 'Philip Green agrees to pay £363 million into BHS pension fund', 28 February 2017, https://www.theguardian.com/business/2017/feb/28/philip-green-agrees-pay-363m-bhs-pension-fund.

25 *Retail Gazette*, 'What happened to you BHS?', 28 April 2016, https://www.retailgazette. co.uk/blog/2016/04/what-happened-to-you-bhs/.

26 Triodos Bank annual report 2017, http://www.annual-report-triodos.com/en/2017/ our-group/about-triodos-bank/key-figures.html.

27 Iain Martin, *Making It Happen: Fred Goodwin, RBS and the Men Who Blew Up the British Economy*, London: Simon & Schuster, 2013.

Chapter 5

1 Philip Crosby, *Quality Is Free*, New York: McGraw-Hill, 1979.

2 Michael Porter, *Competitive Advantage: Creating and Sustaining Superior Performance*, Boston: Harvard Business School Press, 1985.

3 Tata Code of Conduct, p. 5, http://www.tata.com/pdf/tcoc-booklet-2015.pdf.

4 Ibid., p. 7.

5 https://www.mondragon-corporation.com/en/co-operative-experience/our-principles/.

6 Michael E. Brown, Linda K. Treviño and David A. Harrison, 'Ethical Leadership: A Social Learning Perspective for Concept Development and Testing', *Organizational Behavior and Human Design Processes*, 97, 2005, pp. 117–34.

7 Inmaculada Adarves-Yorno, 'The Paradox of Authenticity', in Bolden et al., *Leadership Paradoxes*; Herminia Ibarra, *Act Like a Leader, Think Like a Leader*, Boston: Harvard Business Review Press, 2015.

8 Hatch and Schultz, *Taking Brand Initiative*.

9 https://www.edenproject.com/eden-story/behind-the-scenes/ethical-buying-at-eden.

10 Fu Jia, Jonathan Gosling and Morgen Witzel, *Sustainable Champions: How International Companies Are Changing the Face of Business in China*, Sheffield: Greenleaf, 2015.

11 https://www.mckinsey.com/about-us/overview/our-mission-and-values.

12 Frederick Herzberg, *Work and the Nature of Man*, Cleveland: World Publishing Company, 1966; J. Richard Hackman and Greg R. Oldham, *Work Redesign*, Reading, MA: Addison-Wesley, 1980; Hackman and Oldham, 'Not What It Was, and Not What It Will Be: The Future of Job Design Research', *Journal of Organizational Behavior*, 31, 2010, pp. 463–79.

13 Rob Goffee and Gareth Jones, 'Leading Clever People', *Harvard Business Review*, March 2007, https://hbr.org/2007/03/leading-clever-people.

14 Paul M. Munchinsky, *Psychology Applied to Work*, Summerfield: Hypergraph Press, 2012.

15 Mary Parker Follett, 'Leadership', Rowntree Management Conference lecture, 28 September 1928.

16 https://www.johnlewispartnership.co.uk/about.html.

17 BBC, 'John Lewis rules out float', 20 September 1999, http://news.bbc.co.uk/1/hi/ business/the_company_file/451620.stm.

18 W. Edwards Deming, *Out of the Crisis*, Cambridge, MA: MIT Center for Advanced Engineering Study, 1986.

19 *The Guardian*, 'BP boss admits job on the line over Gulf oil spill', 14 May 2010, https:// www.theguardian.com/business/2010/may/13/bp-boss-admits-mistakes-gulf-oil-spill.

20 *Washington Post*, 'This is the text message sent to MH370 relatives', 24 March 2014, https://www.theguardian.com/business/2010/may/13/bp-boss-admits-mistakes-gulf-oil-spill.

21 *Financial Times*, 'Maple Leaf Food's response to a crisis', 29 April 2013, https://www.ft.com/content/8c8d3668-adb5-11e2-82b8-00144feabdc0.

22 Witzel, *Tata*, p. 150.

23 Ibid., p. 151.

Chapter 6

1 R. Edward Freeman, *Strategic Management: A Stakeholder Approach*, Boston: Pitman, 1984; Robert Phillips, *Stakeholder Theory and Organizational Ethics*, San Francisco, CA: Berrett-Koehler, 2003.

2 Amantha Imber, 'Help Employees Innovate by Giving Them the Right Challenge', *Harvard Business Review*, October 2016, https://hbr.org/2016/10/help-employees-innovate-by-giving-them-the-right-challenge.

3 Herbert C. Kelman, 'Compliance, Identification and Internalization: Three Processes of Attitude Change', *Journal of Conflict Resolution*, 2 (1), 1958, pp. 51–60.

4 David Sirota, Louis A. Mischkind and Michael Irwin Meltzer, 'Why Your Employees Are Losing Motivation', *Harvard Business School Working Knowledge*, 2006, https:// hbswk.hbs.edu/archive/why-your-employees-are-losing-motivation.

5 W.D. Edmonds, *The First Hundred Years, 1848–1948*, Oneida, NY: Oneida Ltd, 1948, p. 8.

6   Eric Lowenthal, 'The Labor Policy of the Oneida Community Ltd', *Journal of Political Economy*, 35, 1927, pp. 114–26; Pierrepont Noyes, *My Father's House: An Oneida Boyhood*, London: John Murray, 1937.

Chapter 7

1   Naomi Klein, *No Logo: Taking Aim at the Brand Bullies*, Toronto: Knopf, 1999.

2   Morgen Witzel, *A History of Management Thought*, London: Routledge, 2nd edn, 2017.

3   Charles Babbage, *The Economy of Machinery and Manufactures*, London: Charles Knight, 1835.

4   Charles Wilson, *The History of Unilever: A Study in Economic Growth and Social Change*, London: Cassell, 1954.

5   *Business Insider*, 'Americans are avoiding romaine lettuce after an outbreak – and it remains one of the most dangerous grocery-store habits', 23 April 2018, http://uk.businessinsider.com/romaine-lettuce-outbreak-reveals-common-food-poisoning-danger-2018-4?r=US&IR=T.

6   Paul T. Cherington, *The Elements of Marketing*, New York: Macmillan, 1920.

7   Piers Brendon, *Thomas Cook: 150 Years of Popular Tourism*, London: Secker & Warburg, 1991; John Pudney, *The Thomas Cook Story*, London: Michael Joseph, 1953.

8   *The Independent*, 'Thomas Cook: From a tragedy to a corporate disaster', 19 May 2015, https://www.independent.co.uk/news/business/analysis-and-features/carbon-monoxide-deaths-from-a-tragedy-to-a-corporate-disaster-for-thomas-cook-10259735.html.

9   Ibid.

10   *Which?* 'Which? Awards 2017 winners revealed', https://www.which.co.uk/news/2017/05/which-awards-2017-winners-revealed/; *Sunday Times*, 'The *Sunday Times* 100 best companies', 26 February 2016, https://appointments.thetimes.co.uk/article/best100companies/.

Chapter 8

1   http://news.gallup.com/poll/1597/Confidence-Institutions.aspx.

2   Witzel, *Tata*.

3 *Forbes*, profile of Martin Winterkorn, n.d., https://www.forbes.com/profile/martin-winterkorn/.

4 *Ars Technica*, 'Volkswagen's emissions cheating scandal has a long, complicated history', 24 September 2017, https://arstechnica.com/cars/2017/09/volkswagens-emissions-cheating-scandal-has-a-long-complicated-history/.

5 *Bloomberg*, 'Ex-VW CEO Winterkorn charged by U.S. in diesel-cheating case', https://www.bloomberg.com/news/articles/2018-05-03/ex-vw-ceo-winterkorn-charged-by-u-s-in-diesel-cheating-case.

6 Witzel, *Tata*.

7 Eduardo Leite, 'Why Trust Matters in Business', World Economic Forum agenda, 19 January 2015, https://www.weforum.org/agenda/2015/01/why-trust-matters-in-business/.

8 Ashok Som, 'Volkswagen in China: Running the Olympic Marathon', *European Business Forum*, 30, 2007, pp. 46–9; Tim Ambler, Morgen Witzel and Chao Xi, *Doing Business in China*, 4th edn, London: Routledge, 2015.

9 Jia, Gosling and Witzel, *Sustainable Champions*.

10 John Styles, *Titus Salt and Saltaire: Industry and Virtue*, Saltaire: Salts Estates, 1990; Ian Campbell Bradley, 'Titus Salt: Enlightened Entrepreneur', *History Today*, 37 (5), 1987, pp. 30–6.

Chapter 9

1 For the ideology of shareholder value maximization, see Alfred Rappaport, *Creating Shareholder Value: The New Standard for Business Performance*, New York: The Free Press, 1986.

2 William Lazonick and Mary O'Sullivan, 'Maximizing Shareholder Value: A New Ideology For Corporate Governance', *Economy and Society*, 29 (1), 2010, pp. 13–35.

3 'Carillion: Second Joint Report from the Business, Energy and Industrial Strategy and Work and Pensions Committees of Session 2017–19', London: House of Commons, 2018, p. 3, https://publications.parliament.uk/pa/cm201719/cmselect/cmworpen/769/769.pdf.

4 Dominic Barton, 'Capitalism for the Long Term', *Harvard Business Review*, March 2011, https://hbr.org/2011/03/capitalism-for-the-long-term.

5 Dominic Barton and Mark Wiseman, 'Focusing Capital on the Long Term', *Harvard Business Review*, December 2013, https://www.mckinsey.com/featured-insights/leadership/focusing-capital-on-the-long-term.

Chapter 10

1 Laura Nash, 'Ethics Without the Sermon', *Harvard Business Review*, November 1981, https://hbr.org/1981/11/ethics-without-the-sermon.

2 Ibid.

3 Ibid.

4 Ibid.

5 Ibid.

6 Ibid.

7 Josephson Institute of Ethics, 'Five Steps of Principled Reasoning', 1999, https://ethicsalarms.com/rule-book/ethical-decision-making-tools/.

8 Friederike Fabritius and Hans W. Hagemann, *The Leading Brain: Neuroscience Hacks to Work Smarter, Better, Happier*, New York: Penguin Random House, 2017.

9 Paul Bloomfield, 'The Harm of Immorality', *Ratio* 21, 2008, pp. 241–59; B. Bastian et al., 'Losing Our Humanity: The Self-Dehumanizing Consequences of Social Ostracism', *Personality and Social Psychology Bulletin*, 39 (2), 2013, pp. 156–69; Eva Tsahuridu, 'How Unethical Behaviour Can Harm Our Health', *Intheblack*, 1 September 2016, https://www.intheblack.com/articles/2016/09/01/how-unethical-behaviour-can-harm-our-health.; Camille S. Johnson, 'Unethical Behaviour Can Become Contagious', *Psychology Today*, 29 June 2012, https://www.psychologytoday.com/us/blog/its-all-relative/201206/unethical-behavior-can-become-contagious.; Maurice E. Schweitzer and David E. Gibson, 'Fairness, Feelings, and Ethical Decision-Making: Consequences of Violating Community Standards of Fairness', *Journal of Business Ethics*, 77, 2008, pp. 287–301.

10 Barbara W. Tuchman, *The Guns of August*, New York: Macmillan, 1962.

11 Michael J. Marquardt, *Optimizing the Power of Action Learning*, London: Nicholas Brealey, 2011.

12 Otto Rank, *Art and Artist: Creative Urge and Personality Development*, New York: W.W. Norton, 1932.

13 Markkula Center for Applied Ethics, 'A Framework for Ethical Decision Making', https://www.scu.edu/ethics/ethics-resources/ethical-decision-making/a-framework-for-ethical-decision-making/.

14 Archie B. Carroll, 'The Pyramid of Corporate Social Responsibility: Toward the Moral Management of Organizational Stakeholders', *Business Horizons*, July–August 1991, pp. 39–48; Kenneth Arrow, *Social Choice and Individual Values*, New York: John Wiley, 1951.

15 Henry Mintzberg, *The Nature of Managerial Work*, New York: Harper & Row, 1973.

16 Susan Klitzman and Jeanne M. Stellman, 'The Impact of the Physical Environment on the Psychological Well-Being of Office Workers', *Social Science and Medicine*, 29 (6), 1989, pp. 733–42.

17 Maryam Kouchaki and Isaac H. Smith, 'The Morning Morality Effect: The Influence of Time of Day on Unethical Behavior', *Psychological Science*, 2013, http://journals. sagepub.com/doi/abs/10.1177/0956797613498099.

18 Laozi, *Daodejiing*.

19 Norman Dixon, *On the Psychology of Military Incompetence*, London: Pimlico, 1976.

Chapter 11

1 Henry Mintzberg, 'Crafting Strategy', *Harvard Business Review*, July 1987, https://hbr. org/1987/07/crafting-strategy/ar/1.

BIBLIOGRAPHY

Adarves-Yorno, Inmaculada (2016) 'The Paradox of Authenticity', in Richard Bolden, Morgen Witzel and Nigel Linacre (eds), *Leadership Paradoxes*, London: Routledge.

Alberts, Robert C. (1973) *The Good Provider: H.J. Heinz and His 57 Varieties*, London: Arthur Barker.

Ambler, Tim, Witzel, Morgen and Xi, Chao (2015) *Doing Business in China*, London: Routledge, 4th edn.

Arrow, Kennth (1951) *Social Choice and Individual Values*, New York: John Wiley.

Auerbach, F. (1903) *The Zeiss Works and the Carl-Zeiss Stiftung in Jena*, trans. S.F. Paul and F.J. Cheshire, London: Marshall, Brookes and Chalkley, 1904.

Babbage, Charles (1835) *The Economy of Machinery and Manufactures*, London: Charles Knight.

Barsh, Joanna, Capozzi, Marla M. and Davidson, Jonathan (2008) 'Leadership and Innovation', *McKinsey Quarterly*, January, https://www.mckinsey.com/business-functions/strategy-and-corporate-finance/our-insights/leadership-and-innovation.

Barton, Dominic (2011) 'Capitalism for the Long Term', *Harvard Business Review*, March, https://hbr.org/2011/03/capitalism-for-the-long-term.

Barton, Dominic and Wiseman, Mark (2013) 'Focusing Capital on the Long Term', *Harvard Business Review*, December, https://www.mckinsey.com/featured-insights/leadership/focusing-capital-on-the-long-term.

Barwise, Patrick and Meehan, Seán (2011) *Beyond the Familiar: Long-Term Growth Through Customer Focus and Innovation*, San Francisco, CA: Jossey-Bass.

Bastian, B. et al. (2013) 'Losing Our Humanity: The Self-Dehumanizing Consequences of Social Ostracism', *Personality and Social Psychology Bulletin* 39 (2): 156–69.

Bateson, John E.G. (1998) *Managing Services Marketing*, Chicago: Dryden.

Bentham, Jeremy (1789) *An Introduction to the Principles of Morals and Legislation*, repr. Oxford: Clarendon, 1996.

Bloomfield, Paul (2008) 'The Harm of Immorality', *Ratio* 21: 241–59.

Board, Jennifer (2016) 'The Paradox of Ethics', in Richard Bolden, Morgen Witzel and Nigel Linacre (eds), *Leadership Paradoxes*, London: Routledge.

Bolden, Richard, Hawkins, Beverley, Gosling, Jonathan and Taylor, Scott (2011) *Exploring Leadership: Individual, Organizational and Societal Perspectives*, Oxford: Oxford University Press.

Bolden, Richard, Witzel, Morgen and Linacre, Nigel (eds) (2016) *Leadership Paradoxes*, London: Routledge.

Bradley, Ian Campbell (1987) 'Titus Salt: Enlightened Entrepreneur', *History Today* 37 (5): 30–6.

Brendon, Piers (1991) *Thomas Cook: 150 Years of Popular Tourism*, London: Secker & Warburg.

Brown, Gerry (2016) *The Independent Director*, Basingstoke: Palgrave Macmillan.

Brown, Michael E., Treviño, Linda K. and Harrison, David A. (2005) 'Ethical Leadership: A Social Learning Perspective for Concept Development and Testing', *Organizational Behavior and Human Design Processes* 97: 117–34.

Buenstorf, Guido and Murmann, Johan Peter (2005) 'Ernst Abbé's Scientific Management: Insights from a Nineteenth-Century Dynamic Capabilities Approach', *Industrial and Corporate Change* 14 (4): 543–74.

Buirski, Peter J., Plutchik, Robert and Kellerman, Henry (1978) 'Sex Differences, Dominance and Personality in the Chimpanzee', *Animal Behaviour* 26 (1): 123–9.

Cadbury, Edward (1912) *Experiments in Industrial Organization*, London: Longmans, Green & Co.

Cahn, Steven M. and Markie, Peter (1998) *Ethics: History, Theory and Contemporary Issues*, Oxford: Oxford University Press.

Carroll, Archie B. (1991) 'The Pyramid of Corporate Social Responsibility: Toward the Moral Management of Organizational Stakeholders', *Business Horizons*, July–August: 39–48.

Chan, W.K.K. (1982) 'The Organizational Structure of the Traditional Chinese Firm and Its Modern Reform', *Business History Review* 56 (2): 218–35; repr. in R. Ampalavanar Brown (ed.), *Chinese Business Enterprise: Critical Perspectives on Business and Management*, London: Routledge, 1982, vol. 1: 216–30.

Chapman, Peter (2010) *The Last of the Imperious Rich*, London: Portfolio Penguin.

Cherington, Paul T. (1920) *The Elements of Marketing*, New York: Macmillan.

Crisp, Roger (2000) *Aristotle: Nicomachean Ethics*, Cambridge: Cambridge University Press.

Crosby, Philip (1979) *Quality Is Free*, New York: McGraw-Hill.

De Roover, Raymond (1955) 'Scholastic Economics: Survival and Lasting Influence from the Sixteenth Century to Adam Smith', *Quarterly Journal of Economics* 69 (2): 161–90; repr. in Mark Blaug (ed.), *St Thomas Aquinas*, Aldershot: Edward Elgar, 1991, 67–96.

Deming, W. Edwards (1986) *Out of the Crisis*, Cambridge, MA: MIT Center for Advanced Engineering Study.

Dewey, John (1901) *Lectures on Ethics*, repr. Carbondale: Southern Illinois University Press, 1991.

Dillan, Jared (2011), *Street Freak: Money and Madness at Lehman Brothers*, New York: Simon & Schuster.

Dixon, Norman (1976) *On the Psychology of Military Incompetence*, London: Pimlico.

Duhamel, Georges (1928) *Scènes de la vie future*, Paris: Éditions Mercure.

Edmonds, W.D. (1948) *The First Hundred Years, 1848–1948* Oneida, New York: Oneida Ltd.

England, E.C.G. (1928) 'The eternal quest', Rowntree Management Conference lecture, 30 September.

Fabritius, Friederike and Hagemann, Hans W. (2017) *The Leading Brain: Neuroscience Hacks to Work Smarter, Better, Happier*, New York: Penguin Random House.

Follett, Mary Parker (1924) *Creative Experience*, New York: Longmans, Green.

Follett, Mary Parker (1928) 'Leadership', Rowntree Management Conference lecture, 28 September.

Freeman, R. Edward (1984) *Strategic Management: A Stakeholder Approach*, Boston: Pitman.

Fried, Charles (1978) *Right and Wrong*, Cambridge, MA: Harvard University Press.

Friedman, Milton (1992) *Capitalism and Freedom*, Chicago: University of Chicago Press.

Furtner, Marco R., Maran, Thomas and Rauthman, John F. (2017) 'Dark Leadership: The Role of Leaders' Dark Triad Personality Traits', in Matthew G. Clark and Craig W. Gruber (eds), *Leadership Development Deconstructed*, New York: Springer, pp. 75–99.

Gerstner, Louis (2002) *Who Says Elephants Can't Dance? Leading a Great Enterprise Through Dramatic Change*, New York: HarperCollins.

Glover, Jonathan (ed.) (1990) *Utilitarianism and Its Critics*, New York: Macmillan.

Goffee, Rob and Jones, Gareth (2007) 'Leading Clever People', *Harvard Business Review*, March, https://hbr.org/2007/03/leading-clever-people.

Greely, Henry (1992) *The Code of Codes: Scientific and Social Issues in the Human Genome Project*, Cambridge, MA: Harvard University Press.

Greulich, Peter E. (2014) *A View from Beneath the Dancing Elephant: Rediscovering IBM's Corporate Constitution*, New York: MBI Concepts.

Hackman, J. Richard and Oldham, Greg R. (1980) *Work Redesign*, Reading, MA: Addison-Wesley.

Hackman, J. Richard and Oldham, Greg R. (2010) 'Not What It Was, and Not What It Will Be: The Future of Job Design Research', *Journal of Organizational Behavior* 31: 463–79.

Haskins, Gay, Thomas, Mike and Johri, Lalit (eds) (2018) *Kindness in Leadership*, London: Routledge.

Hatch, Mary Jo and Schultz, Majken (2008) *Taking Brand Initiative: How Companies Can Align Strategy, Culture and Identity Through Corporate Branding*, Chichester: John Wiley.

Heck, Gene W. (2004) *Islam Inc.: An Early Business History*, Riyadh: King Faisal Center for Research and Islamic Studies.

Hertzke, Alan D. and McRorie, Chris (1998) 'The Concept of Moral Ecology', in Peter Lawler and Dale McConkey (eds), *Community and Political Thought Today*, Westport, CT: Praeger.

Herzberg, Frederick (1966) *Work and the Nature of Man*, Cleveland, OH: World Publishing Company.

Huan-Chang, Chen (1911) *The Economic Princples of Confucius and His School*, New York: Longmans, Green; repr. Bristol: Thoemmes Press, 2002.

Ibarra, Herminia (2015) *Act Like a Leader, Think Like a Leader*, Boston: Harvard Business Review Press.

Ibn Khaldun (1986) *The Muqaddimah*, trans. Franz Rosenthal, London: Routledge.

Imai, Masaaki (1996) *Kaizen: The Key to Japan's Competitive Success*, New York: Random House.

Imber, Amantha (2016) 'Help Employees Innovate By Giving Them the Right Challenge', *Harvard Business Review*, October, https://hbr.org/2016/10/help-employees-innovate-by-giving-them-the-right-challenge.

James, William (1907) *Pragmatism: A New Name for Some Old Ways of Thinking*, New York: Longmans, Green.

Jia, Fu, Gosling, Jonathan and Witzel, Morgen (2015) *Sustainable Champions: How International Companies Are Changing the Face of Business in China*, Sheffield: Greenleaf.

Johnson, Camille S. (2012) 'Unethical Behaviour Can Become Contagious', *Psychology Today*, 29 June, https://www.psychologytoday.com/us/blog/its-all-relative/201206/unethical-behavior-can-become-contagious.

Johnson, Luke (2014) 'Lies, Damned Lies and Running a Business', *Financial Times*, 30 September, http://www.ft.com/cms/s/0/364f2924-47e1-11e4-ac9f-00144feab7de. html#axzz3FH4CKRWx.

Josephson Institute of Ethics (1999) 'Five Steps of Principled Reasoning', https://ethicsalarms.com/rule-book/ethical-decision-making-tools/.

Kant, Immanuel (1785) *Groundwork of the Metaphysics of Morals*, New York: Harper & Row, 1964.

Kelman, Herbert C. (1958) 'Compliance, Identification and Internalization: Three Processes of Attitude Change', *Journal of Conflict Resolution* 2 (1): 51–60.

Kim, W. Chan and Mauborgne, Renée (2005) *Blue Ocean Strategy: How to Create Uncontested Market Space and Make the Competition Irrelevant*, Boston: Harvard Business School Press.

Klein, Naomi (1999) *No Logo: Taking Aim at the Brand Bullies*, Toronto: Knopf.

Klitzman, Susan and Stellman, Jeanne M. (1989) 'The Impact of the Physical Environment on the Psychological Well-Being of Office Workers', *Social Science and Medicine* 29 (6): 733–42.

Kotter, John P. (1990) *A Force for Change: How Leadership Differs from Management*, New York: The Free Press.

Kotter, John P. (1996) *Leading Change*, Boston: Harvard Business School Press.

Kouchaki, Maryam and Smith, Isaac H. (2013) 'The Morning Morality Effect: The Influence of Time of Day on Unethical Behavior', *Psychological Science*, http://journals.sagepub.com/doi/abs/10.1177/0956797613498099.

Laozi (1990) *Daodejing*, trans. John C.H. Wu, London: Shambhala.

Lawlor, John and Gold, Jeff (2016) 'XXXX', in Richard Bolden, Morgen Witzel and Nigel Linacre (eds), *Leadership Paradoxes*, London: Routledge.

Lazonick, William and O'Sullivan, Mary (2010) 'Maximizing Shareholder Value: A New Ideology for Corporate Governance', *Economy and Society* 29 (1): 13–35.

Lee, John (1923) 'The ethics of industry', Rowntree Management Conference lecture, 23 September.

Leite, Eduardo (2015) 'Why Trust Matters in Business', World Economic Forum agenda, 19 January, https://www.weforum.org/agenda/2015/01/why-trust-matters-in-business/.

Levitt, Steven D. and Dubner, Stephen J. (2005) *Freakonomics*, New York: William Morrow.

Levitt, Theodore (1960) 'Marketing Myopia', *Harvard Business Review*, https://hbr.org/2004/07/marketing-myopia.

Lewis, John Spedan (1954) *Fairer Shares*, London: Staples Press.

Lowenthal, Eric (1927) 'The Labor Policy of the Oneida Community Ltd.', *Journal of Political Economy* 35: 114–26.

Lowes-Dickinson, Arthur (1924) 'The necessity for greater publicity in management accounts', Rowntree Management Conference lecture, 25 September.

Macintyre, Alasdair (1998) *A Short History of Ethics: A History of Moral Philosophy from the Homeric Age to the Twentieth Century*, London: Routledge.

Markkula Center for Applied Ethics, 'A Framework for Ethical Decision Making', https://www.scu.edu/ethics/ethics-resources/ethical-decision-making/a-framework-for-ethical-decision-making/.

Marquardt, Michael J. (2011) *Optimizing the Power of Action Learning*, London: Nicholas Brealey.

Martin, Iain (2013) *Making It Happen: Fred Goodwin, RBS and the Men Who Blew Up the British Economy*, London: Simon & Schuster.

Mill, John Stuart (1861) *Utilitarianism*, repr. Oxford: Clarendon, 1998.

Mintzberg, Henry (1973) *The Nature of Managerial Work*, New York: Harper & Row.

Mintzberg, Henry (1987) 'Crafting Strategy', *Harvard Business Review*, July, https://hbr.org/1987/07/crafting-strategy/ar/1.

Monk, Ray (2012) *Robert Oppenheimer: A Life Inside the Center*, New York: Doubleday.

Munchinsky, Paul, M. (2012) *Psychology Applied to Work*, Summerfield, FL: Hypergraph Press.

Nash, Laura (1981) 'Ethics Without the Sermon', *Harvard Business Review*, November, https://hbr.org/1981/11/ethics-without-the-sermon.

Nayak, Ajit (2016) 'Wisdom and the Tragic Question: Moral Learning and Emotional Perception in Leadership and Organisations', *Journal of Business Ethics* 137: 1–13.

Nayar, Vineet (2010) *Employees First, Customers Second: Turning Conventional Management Upside Down*, Boston: Harvard Business Review Press.

Noyes, Pierrepont (1937) *My Father's House: An Oneida Boyhood*, London: John Murray.

Ohmae, Kenichi (1982) *The Mind of the Strategist*, New York: McGraw-Hill.

Perpich, Diane (2008) *The Ethics of Emmanuel Levinas*, Stanford, CA: Stanford University Press.

Phillips, Robert (2003) *Stakeholder Theory and Organizational Ethics*, San Francisco, CA: Berrett-Koehler.

Porter, Michael (1985) *Competitive Advantage: Creating and Sustaining Superior Performance*, Boston: Harvard Business School Press.

Prabhupada, A.C. and Swami, Bhaktivedante (ed. and trans.) (1972) *Bhagavad-Gita As It Is*, New York: Collier.

Pudney, John (1953) *The Thomas Cook Story*, London: Michael Joseph.

Radjou, Navi, Prabu, Jaideep and Ahuja, Simone (2012) *Jugaad Innovation: Think Frugal, Be Flexible, Generate Breakthrough Growth*, Chichester: Wiley.

Rank, Otto (1932) *Art and Artist: Creative Urge and Personality Development*, New York: W.W. Norton.

Rappaport, Alfred (1986) *Creating Shareholder Value: The New Standard for Business Performance*, New York: The Free Press.

Rawls, John (1971) *A Theory of Justice*, New York: Belknap.

Resick, Christian J., Hanges, Paul J., Dickson, Marcus W. and Mitchelson, Jacqueline K. (2006) 'A Cross-Cultural Examination of the Endorsement of Ethical Leadership', *Journal of Business Ethics* 63: 345–59.

Robbins, Lionel (1935) *An Essay on the Nature and Significance of Economic Science*, London: Macmillan.

Ross, W.D. (1930) *The Right and the Good*, Oxford: Clarendon.

Schweitzer, Maurice E. and Gibson, David E. (2008) 'Fairness, Feelings, and Ethical Decision-Making: Consequences of Violating Community Standards of Fairness', *Journal of Business Ethics* 77: 287–301.

Segal, Ronald (1995) *The Black Diaspora*, New York: Farrar, Strauss and Giroux.

Semler, Ricardo (1993) *Maverick*, New York: Warner Books.

Sen, Amartya (1987) *On Ethics and Economics*, Oxford: Blackwell.

Sheldon, Oliver (1923) *The Philosophy of Management*, London: Pitman.

Sirota, David, Mischkind, Louis A. and Meltzer, Michael Irwin (2006) 'Why Your Employees Are Losing Motivation', Harvard Business School Working Knowledge, https://hbswk.hbs.edu/archive/why-your-employees-are-losing-motivation.

Slote, Michael (ed.) (2010) *Essays on the History of Ethics*, Oxford: Oxford University Press.

Smith, Adam (1759) *The Theory of Moral Sentiments*, Edinburgh; repr. London: Forgotten Books, 2010.

Som, Ashok (2007) 'Volkswagen in China: Running the Olympic Marathon', *European Business Forum* 30: 46–9.

Styles, John (1990) *Titus Salt and Saltaire: Industry and Virtue*, Saltaire: Salts Estates.

Tolstoy, Leo (1869), *War and Peace*, trans. Rosemary Edmonds, London: Penguin, 1957.

Tsahuridu, Eva (2016) 'How Unethical Behaviour Can Harm Our Health', *Intheblack*, 1 September, https://www.intheblack.com/articles/2016/09/01/how-unethical-behaviour-can-harm-our-health.

Tuchman, Barbara W. (1962) *The Guns of August*, New York: Macmillan.

Watson, Burton (1964) *Han Fei Tzu: Basic Writings*, New York: Columbia University Press.

Watson, Burton (2007) *The Analects of Confucius*, New York: Columbia University Press.

Whitehead, Thomas North (1936) *Leadership in a Free Society*, London: Oxford University Press.

Wilson, Charles (1954) *The History of Unilever: A Study in Economic Growth and Social Change*, London: Cassell.

Witzel, Morgen (2008) *Tata: The Evolution of a Corporate Brand*, New Delhi: Penguin India.

Witzel, Morgen (2012) 'The Leadership Philosophy of Han Fei', *Asia Pacific Business Review* 18 (4): 1–15.

Witzel, Morgen (2016) *Managing For Success: Spotting Signs of Corporate Failure and Fixing Them Before They Happen*, London: Bloomsbury.

Witzel, Morgen (2017) *A History of Management Thought*, London: Routledge, 2nd edn.

Wood, Allan W. (2005) 'Kant's History of Ethics', *Studies in the History of Ethics*, June, http://www.historyofethics.org/062005/062005Wood.shtml.

Zak, Paul J. (2004) 'Neuronomics', *Philosophical Transactions of the Royal Society, B: Biological Sciences* 359: 1737–48.

Zak, Paul J. (2012) *The Moral Molecule: The Source of Love and Prosperity*, New York: Dutton.

Zeithaml, Valarie (2007) *Driving Customer Equity: How Customer Lifetime Value Is Reshaping Corporate Strategy*, Boston: Harvard Business School Press.

INDEX